The Wizards of Consciousness

Making the Imponderable Practical

D1089616

BY LYNDA MADDEN DAHL

Beyond the Winning Streak
Using Conscious Creation to
Consistently Win at Life

Ten Thousand Whispers
A Guide to Conscious Creation

The Wizards of Consciousness
Making the Imponderable Practical

Lynda Dahl's books are available on
audiocassette through bookstores,
Seth Network International
and The Woodbridge Group

The Wizards of Consciousness

Making the Imponderable Practical

Lynda Madden Dahl

The Woodbridge Group

The Wizards of Consciousness

Copyright © 1997 by Lynda Madden Dahl
Author photo copyright © 1997 by Stan Ulkowski
Cover design copyright © 1997 by The Woodbridge Group

Published in the United States of America. All rights reserved. For reproduction and use permission, contact The Woodbridge Group.

First printing, May 1997

Library of Congress Cataloging-in-Publication Data
Dahl, Lynda Madden, 1943—
   The wizards of consciousness: making the imponderable practical / by Lynda Madden Dahl
      p.   cm.
   Includes bibliographical references.
   ISBN 1-889964-03-4 (pbk.) : $13.95
   1. Mental suggestion—Miscellanea. 2. Consciousness—Miscellanea. 3. Seth (Spirit). I. Title.
BF1156.S8D35 1997
131—dc21   96-49174
                                                                             CIP

The Woodbridge Group
PO Box 849 ✦ Eugene OR ✦ 97440 ✦ USA
(541) 683-6731 ✦ fax (541) 683-1084

In Dedication

This book is dedicated to the people who eschew conventional world thinking and strike out on their own to discover the nature of consciousness—the people who push the envelope of ideas far beyond the sanctioned, through their intense desire to know more and to experience more. This book is dedicated to the wizards of consciousness.

L.M.D.

◆ ◆ ◆

In Appreciation

To Seth, Jane and Rob: A day seldom passes that I don't silently offer my appreciation to you for the material you brought to the world, and the intense focus it took to make it happen. Where would we be today without your priceless commitment?

To Stan: Thank goodness you haven't changed in one important regard since we fell in love ages ago—you staunchly support me in whatever I undertake. I can't imagine having written this book, or lived my life, without you.

To Matt and Cathleen: You became the harbingers of major change for me by the simple acts of your births. In important ways, what I think today is due to you, my dears.

To Katharine Newcomb, Sheri LoBello and Mary Barton: You not only helped me create the writing time needed to finish this book through your daily assistance with my work commitments, you offered ongoing support as well. Thank you, my friends.

To Suzanne Delisle and Katharine Newcomb: My esteem for you as editors of *Wizards* is only superseded by my esteem for you as friends, which you know is very significant.

To Melissa and Rocky Langeliers: Your lovely home on the Oregon coast afforded me the peace and solitude I needed to write a good portion of this book. My appreciation is sincere.

Contents

Where your physical survival...once depended upon a narrowed focus while you learned physical manipulation, now the success of that manipulation necessitates a broadening of focus—a new awakening into the larger existence of the selfhood...

—*Seth*, The "Unknown" Reality, Volume One, *Session 686*

Introduction

Oh, my gawd! I thought. *Now you've done it. Let's see how you psychically wiggle out of this one.* It had been two hours since I'd returned to my New York City hotel room after a leisurely breakfast, and I was headed out the door for my first appointment of the day. As I searched the desktop for my room key, it hit me—I'd left it in the outside lock when I'd entered the room after tea and a croissant that morning. I opened the door and studied the empty key slot, and knew I had choices to make.

In days of old, there would have been no option except to ask that I be moved to another room immediately. Now, things were different. Times had changed. I had changed. Now I knew one of my choices was to get on with my day, not worry about the missing key, and simply feel at home in a safe universe.

Oh, right. Midtown New York does have a slight reputation, remember? So you don't lock your home or car—the Northwest this isn't. Yeah, but I'm me. I don't change just because my location changes. I take my security with me, as long as I believe in it.

And therein lay my dilemma. Did I <u>believe</u> New York was as safe for me as Oregon? How had I felt the previous day on my cab ride in from La Guardia? What thoughts had registered that night when I had considered leaving the hotel at midnight for a stroll? How had I felt on previous trips into the city, about its people, its atmosphere, its attitude?

Somewhat uneasy, I uneasily admitted. Were my off-center feelings enough to set the stage for personal grief? I wondered. Or, if I used the magical approach to life, the approach I'm supposed to be learning, could I stay in my present room and walk away unscathed three days later when I departed for Washington, D.C.?

It only took seconds to collect my thoughts and sense of personal safety around me like a familiar cloak. As soon as I made the decision to continue my stay in the room and simply request a replacement key from the front desk, I felt solid again. Only once or twice during the remainder of my time in New York did I fleetingly wonder what had happened to the key. But never again did I feel a sense of unease.

Until I got to D.C., that is, and promptly lost my American Express card, followed the next day by my Visa. *What the heck's going on!* I asked my inner self. "*Well,*" it replied in all its wisdom, "*you're experimenting with creation, so experiment away. Only tuck a quarter into your shoe in case you choose to lose your purse and have to make a phone call.*"

Very funny, oh great spirit guide. Very funny, unless you're on the receiving end of such events, then they become Learning Experiences. That's capital L, capital E: those events most people would rather do without. But life is a Learning Experience and there's no way around it, so I decided I'd better make the best of two more uneasy situations.

I pulled my fraying security cloak about me, and decided I'd not consider the whereabouts of either card with trepidation. I'd use the magical approach to life, the approach I'm supposed to be learning, and assume nothing of ill import would come of the loss of either card. And it didn't.

Good-Bye Mainstream

Metaphysics has changed my life. While my anecdotal slant on the lost objects mentioned above has been brushed lightly with humor, the impact of what occurred is anything but light. Many facets of metaphysics come into play when any event is experienced, and a structure that supports the creation of an event becomes obvious after studying metaphysics for awhile. At least the brand of metaphysics explained by Jane Roberts and Seth.

If you have never heard of Jane and Seth, you were probably flowing with mainstream America during the 1970s and early 1980s during their tremendous popularity. Although "New Age" seems old hat nowadays, the term wasn't even coined when Seth made his appearance in this reality in the early 1960s. In fact, it's been suggested that the combined writings of Jane Roberts and Seth launched that era of broader thought that moved so many out of the conventional flow and into new understandings quite at odds with most of the world's accepted beliefs.

In 1963 Jane, a young woman and respected author, decided to write a book on extrasensory perception. As part of her research into the subject, she and her husband Robert F. Butts borrowed a Ouija board from a friend to get a feel for the mystical lay of the land. As their fingers touched the plastic pointer, it slowly moved toward letter after letter of the alphabet printed on the board's surface. After several sessions the pointer picked up speed and started quickly moving between the letters. The letters formed words and words sentences, and sentences formed a conversation with an entity who called himself Seth, an "energy personality essence."

Within ten or so sessions on the Ouija board, Jane had the urge to speak for Seth. Eventually she dropped enough of her concerns and inhibitions to let Seth use her voice and persona to communicate his words around the world. While Jane's psyche moved out of the way, many times leaving her without a clue as to what was said during the time Seth was talking through her, Rob took hand-written notes. Jane logged over 4,000 hours in trance, resulting in over 1,800 transcribed sessions over twenty-plus years.

Seth dictated verbatim ten books during that time, and Jane wrote another 15 of her own concurrently with Seth's works-in-progress.[1] An almost equal body of work still awaits publication: sessions originally deleted from book material for various reasons (including personal information given Rob and Jane), and transcriptions of ESP class sessions Jane held for many years. An estimated seven to ten million people have read—and many of those constantly re-read— the combined works of these two incredibly brilliant thinkers, work that is now archived at Yale University, the only metaphysical material accepted by Yale to date.

Statistics, however, only tell a small part of the Seth/Jane Roberts phenomenon. Most important, lives have been forever changed because of the impact of the material on people's thinking. Certainly mine was. I read my first Seth book in 1984, and after a period of hesitation about jumping from the comforting banks of mainstream into the foo-foo waters of metaphysics, I never looked back. Thank goodness.

The Secret Life of Thought

The message that weaves so eloquently through the Seth material is that each of us is consciousness which *chose* to be born into physical reality for our own reasons. Our lives have great meaning and purpose because we planned to come here to experience the translation of our thoughts, feelings and beliefs into events. The now common Seth quote, "You create your own reality," turns the world's ideas upside down and inside out because it suggests that the cause of events is within each of us, not generated by outside forces such as randomness, luck, fate, other people or circumstances beyond our control.

Seth says thoughts take on a life of their own after they're created. They join with others of like nature and eventually, if enough thoughts and feelings are generated along the same lines, they form an event that dutifully enters our existence as a life experience. That experience may be an interaction with other people, a material object we wish to own or see, an emotion we want to feel, or any other kind of happening. In fact, *any* event we experience, from the walk down the driveway to secure our morning newspaper, to the walk down the aisle to join our beloved in matrimony, had to be thought or felt into existence, or we simply would not have experienced it. There is no moment of the day that is excluded from this statement, no event that falls outside its parameters. If we experienced it, we created it. End of story.

Well, not quite. For most readers of the Seth material, that statement signals the beginning of their search for understanding. The ones who hold no curiosity about the metaphysics behind creation usually set the books aside and move on to other topics that catch their attention. The ones who stay with Seth long enough to start the questions flowing seldom leave for other, less complicated ground, because other ground doesn't seem to grow answers to seeded questions with the depth that Seth readers come to expect.

And the questions seldom stop. If we create each experience, *how* do we do it? *Why* do we do it? What makes it possible? How do we change what we don't like about our lives? How do we enhance what we do enjoy in our lives? What gives simple, everyday thought the power to create events? What assistance, if any, do we receive from sources outside our known time and space? And what does any of this have to do with consciousness?

Seth answers these questions and hundreds of others, including ones we hadn't previously thought to ask, and he answers them without the trappings of dogma or the distortions created by stuffing new concepts into very, very old thought boxes. Expect fresh, intelligent, clear ideas when you pick up any of Jane Roberts's books. You won't be disappointed or disillusioned, and you just may find information that strikes enough of a chord with you that you set about consciously changing your life based on newly redefined personal desires, intents and purposes.

Choices Unparalleled

It's called conscious creation, and it's all about how we can indeed use our inherent abilities as consciousness in physical form to decide what we want to experience, and then make it happen through focused intent. I've done it, as I told my readers in the two books I've written on the subject, and I know many others who have, also. We've stopped illnesses, made money, changed weather patterns, brought love into our lives, found fulfillment however we chose to define it. Because we're pioneers and not experts, we hit our private walls at times, but at least we're trying. We're breaking ground, connecting dots of understanding for others. We see the big picture, thanks to Seth, Jane and Rob, but we're not always adept at maneuvering within it. But give us an A for effort.

Part of our problem is that we're dealing with concepts that are completely foreign to most people and heresy to others, and it's tough to keep the faith at times in light of more standard world thinking. One of Seth's main ideas is that consciousness gives birth to everything; that is, consciousness is always in place first, followed by what it creates: matter, events, nature, creatures, universes—like we said, everything. If conscious creation is viable, consciousness *must* be in place first—and we must be consciousness. Seth says that we are literal extensions of the consciousness of All That Is, and as such are imbued with the same characteristics as All That Is, including the ability to create with our thoughts. He says we have been given the greatest gift of all...the gift of the gods...the gift of creativity.

Yet the ability to consciously create events and material objects is believed impossible within the theories of classical science, most theologies and most branches of psychology. Conscious creation seems impossible within these thought systems because none of them recognize the role consciousness plays in creating and sustaining physical reality. *And yet many of us have purposely, consciously used our thoughts to bring about desires of choice.*

Rethinking the Scheme of Things

Personally, I'm weary of being told by the prevalent world thought systems that I'm powerless. They say it in nice ways, but the message is clear—and constant. Well, what if they're wrong? What if they have the whole picture turned inside out and misunderstand the message because they are viewing it from the back of the canvas? What if their theories and postulations are based on incorrect readings of physical reality because they're missing the point that brings everything into clear focus? Indeed, what would happen to their theories if they believed that consciousness is all there is and from it, via thought, springs everything else? What would happen? The world would change.

We would, individually and as a whole, start to understand the genesis of events, and we would learn to create experiences worthy of our godly status. We'd stop unwittingly using our power of thought to cause personal and global disasters, and get on with creating lives of worthiness filled with value. Gee whiz, we might even figure out the real purpose of physical reality and what we're supposed to learn about the power of consciousness.

In *Ten Thousand Whispers: A Guide to Conscious Creation* and *Beyond the Winning Streak: Using Conscious Creation to Consistently Win at Life*, I looked at the subject of consciousness from a practical point of view. I laid the groundwork for why conscious creation is possible, and then focused on techniques and suggestions that might help readers create what they wish, and stories that told how others had done it. I call those books my personal chapters one and two of consciousness, or consciousness learning to understand itself.

As my comprehension grows I realize there is more to know, more to decipher, more to explore. This book, then, becomes my own personal chapter three, the chapter in which, by writing about it, I seek to understand more about consciousness, its purpose, its structure, its scope, and its integration into our physical reality. In the back of my mind the idea continually flashes that if we know enough about consciousness, we'll know how to lead fulfilling, satisfying, abundant, loving lives—consciously and consistently. And that, Alfie, is what it's all about.

This is not a book about conscious creation per se, or the how-tos of the subject. It's more a look at consciousness in general, and physically attuned consciousness in particular. Of course, any discussion of consciousness leads us to answers about how to use our creative powers to knowingly shape the individual moments of our lives into one heck of a whole, and hopefully this book is no exception. Through new understandings we will come to terms with who we are, where we're going, and how to get there with ease.

To study consciousness means we must look at it with clear eyes and unmuddied beliefs. And to do that necessitates a step outside the rigorous doctrines and dogmas of accepted world thought, since few if any such systems acknowledge the existence of consciousness. Unofficial, unsanctioned sources of information, then, are our textbooks for this step in our learning.

And, believe me, the information sources for this book's trek through consciousness are *very* unsanctioned. We're over the edge and knee-deep in unconventional thought here—thankfully. As I said in *Ten Thousand Whispers*, mainstream thinking hasn't exactly brought peace on earth and abundance for all, so maybe it's time to set aside, or at least question, the assumptions underlying conventional ideas. And the paradox is we can't question the conventional point of view from the conventional point of view.

Yeah, we're over the edge, and maybe, just maybe, we'll find enough answers and insights from the unsanctioned to eventually understand what a nice bunch of people like you and me are doing here in the first place.

1

Freed by death from the conventional frameworks of thought and belief that surrounded me, I have gained in death insights and comprehensions of the greatest consequence. Ironically, I wonder why these did not come to me in physical life, where certainly I could have put them to as good a use—particularly when it is obvious that they were as available in life as in death—and I am convinced that only certain beliefs and attitudes of mind made these insights psychologically invisible.

—William James, The Afterdeath Journal of an American Philosopher, *Chapter 1*

The Straight Scoop From a Dead William James

Jane Roberts was a fascinating woman. One of the great mystics of our times, her abilities didn't stop with "channeling" Seth. Over the twenty-plus years of her interaction with Seth, which lasted until just days before her death in September 1984, she was able to cultivate openings in her psyche that few in today's world can match, let alone grasp. One such opening led her to tap into the world view of different personalities after they had physically died. She wrote three books that way, using the words of the personalities themselves to tell their own stories, filling page after page with writings that seemed to come from sources very much alive, yet dead in our terms.[1]

One such book is *The Afterdeath Journal of an American*

Philosopher: The World View of William James. James, the world-renowned philosopher, died in 1910. If Seth is correct, William James's world view is "available" for study—just as ours is—if we know how to access it. Jane had the psychic tools and proclivity to do just that. Seth says, "(Jane) was not directly in communication with William James. (She) was aware, however, of the universe through William James's world view. As you might dial a program on a television set, (Jane) tuned in to the view of reality now held in the mind of William James...Each person has such a world view, whether living or dead in your terms, and that 'living picture' exists despite time or space. It <u>can</u> be perceived by others."[2]

What occurred, in essence, was that Jane's everyday self stepped aside and her greater psyche, or consciousness, connected in some way to the world view held by William James. James was then able, in his rather formal yet open manner, to talk about his life in the twentieth century and what his life is like now, after supposed death.

Afterdeath Journal takes the reader on a trip through psychological and spiritual arenas mapped with such brilliance they could only have been traveled by consciousness no longer in physical form. William James presents us with a multidimensional living panorama of consciousness and how its motivations create its existence; how its life continues through discard after discard of physical body; how its learning is assimilated after each such discard; how choices are made to address specific areas of necessary development; and how the exploration of its learning is continued in the greater realms of its existence outside time and space.

James doesn't discover universal laws upon his death, tenets chiseled in clouds awaiting human organization to preserve them. What he does find is a complex interaction of very much alive consciousness exploring its potential. Although by nature James is a philosopher, his observations are not philosophically obtuse. He describes the conditions of his existence, and his perceptions and understandings with an equal sense of serious consideration and self-directed humor. And by so doing, we discover the answers to questions most of humanity thinks unanswerable until after death, if then.

God Redefined

Take God, for example. James says, "Nowhere have I encountered the furnishings of a conventional heaven, or glimpsed the face of God. On the other hand, certainly I dwell in a psychological heaven by earth's standards, for everywhere I sense a presence, or atmosphere, or atmospheric presence that is well-intentioned, gentle yet powerful, and all-knowing. This seems to be a psychological presence of such stunning parts, however, that I can point to no one place and identify it as being there in contrast to being someplace else. At the risk of understating, this presence seems more like a loving condition that permeates existence, and from which all existence springs...All theological and intellectual theories are beside the point in the reality of this phenomenon."[3]

That refreshing description of God starts James's trek through a discussion of this atmospheric presence, or loving condition, or intelligent light, and what it means to experience it. He says he knows that from this presence comes everything, that it forms itself into you and me, and James and others like him, not of the earth. All personalities emerge from it yet remain a part of it. "It is as if the universe were a multidimensional cloth with infinite patterns, and figures which did not remain flat but sprang alive, lived, moved, and died and came alive again, while the fabric of which they were made never wore out but miraculously revitalized itself and rewove its parts."[4]

Does God have human emotions? Not as such, according to James, yet its nature is one of exuberance and its basis is loving intent. It holds within itself what James calls a "well-intentioned quality" that makes him feel completely safe no matter what the conditions of his immediate experience. In trying to grasp the deeper significance of the atmospheric presence, James says it is not an entity, for it is everywhere at once, at every hypothetical point in the universe, yet it is still aware and responsive. He feels sure it "possesses a psychology far divorced from any with which I have ever been acquainted..."

These characteristics of All That Is suggest a sensitive, thinking being or field of consciousness. This is not to say that All That Is thinks and feels in the same manner as its human offspring, which it graces with mind, the ability to analyze and the means to translate interpretations into feelings. All That Is doesn't need such machinations; its methods of psychological manipulation are far greater than that.

A "psychological growing medium" is how James describes All That Is. He says the atmospheric presence seems to promote psychic growth "to the most advantageous degree," and in general creates the conditions most conducive to psychological expansion by consciousness, especially the sense of freedom. All of the qualities necessary for the creation and sustenance of life are found in the atmospheric presence—but that's no big surprise, is it?

Perhaps this quote of James's sums up or rounds out a definition of All That Is that many of us have felt, but never put to words: "I theorize at times that it is the combined consciousness of the entire universe by whatever description, existing within all consciousness, yet apart. At the same time, I am sure that more is involved. Nevertheless, in this (intelligent) light the conditions of existence are the most supportive and encouraging imaginable."[5]

Infinite Consciousness

William James gives us the beginnings of a redefinition of God, based on his perspective after death, and through this redefinition we start to sense or form answers to questions asked by humans through time immemorial. Is there life after death? Does the soul exist? Is there purpose behind each individual life? Are we born again and again into physical existence? Is there a nonphysical power that offers guidance and assistance? Interestingly, the answers to these questions are found by studying consciousness.

What William James says about consciousness comes from one man's sense and knowledge. He views it through his subjective reality and extrapolates conclusions from that experience. And, according to Seth, James is right on. And, according to Seth, there is much more to the story. In fact, the subject of consciousness permeates all of Seth's and Jane's books—no wonder, given that from consciousness all else springs. William James led us to the unconventional edge and we stepped over in our explorations of consciousness and All That Is, so we may as well throw caution to the wind and continue our discussion from Seth's otherworldly standpoint.

According to Seth, "There is no personal God-individual in Christian terms, and yet you do have access to a portion of *All That Is*, a portion highly attuned to you...There is a portion of *All That Is* directed and focused within each individual, residing within each consciousness. Each consciousness is, therefore, cherished and individually protected... These connections between you and *All That Is* can never be severed, and Its awareness is so delicate and focused that Its attention is indeed directed with a prime creator's love to each consciousness."[6]

All That Is is an energy gestalt[7] of such enormous proportions and significance that we can't wrap our minds around the concept. In an indescribably magnificent burst of desire and intent, All That Is created individualized consciousness from its whole. These divine fragments of All That Is were given life of their own so that All That Is, through them, could experience every possible nuance of creation. All That Is, in essence, bade them go experience everything they possibly could. Because they are and always will be a part of All That Is, though individual, what those divine fragments experience (read create) is known and shared by All That Is. That, in fact, is the point of their existence. All That Is, through parts of itself, continues to grow as they do, and it is fulfilled through its own personal creations and the creations of individualized consciousnesses.

Everything that can ever transpire in our universe or beyond emerges from All That Is, or consciousness. So, where does consciousness reside? Everywhere. Nothing can be separate from the fabric of consciousness. It's an impossibility. Consciousness is all that is, All That Is is consciousness. According to Seth, "Consciousness did not come from atoms and molecules scattered by chance through the universe, or scattered by chance through many universes. Consciousness did not arrive because inert matter suddenly soared into activity and song. The consciousness existed first, and evolved the form into which it then began to manifest itself...No form of matter, however potent, will be self-evolved into consciousness, no matter what other bits of matter are added to it."[8]

Consciousness is mental, psychological and psychic. It has no native form that identifies it as consciousness, nothing that one can point to and say, see, there it is...that's consciousness. It exists as pure energy that experiences whatever it wishes to explore. Individualized consciousness does, however, join with other individualized consciousnesses to form groupings and systems, from nonphysical gestalts to human beings, from three-dimensional realities to ones beyond our comprehension—but there really is no separation between these or any other formations and All That Is. The energy of All That Is sustains all of its creations, whether they have an obvious form or no noticeable pattern. If All That Is were to withdraw its energy, the formations could not exist. So there is a literal, not just spiritual, tie between creator and creation.

In order to experience all nuances of expression and learn from them, individualized consciousness has to know intimately what is happening within the whole. Therefore, consciousness can be and is everywhere at once, within time and outside of time simultaneously. It is not fettered by the boundaries of time and space—consciousness *creates* those boundaries—as well as the realities they define.

Since all consciousness is actually one skein, whatever happens to any of its parts is instantaneously known to the rest. Nothing can happen to any consciousness without the whole universe knowing in detail what occurred. Every thought, every movement is immediately know to All That Is and to all that is. There are no secrets, it seems, and no separations in the fullest sense of the words.

If consciousness chooses to take on physical form, then it must conform to the obvious structures that support physical reality. It will, for instance, create a body for itself and then pretend that body is not part of a greater existence; indeed, not part of consciousness at all. That's quite a joke, though, because a body is pure consciousness which molded itself into a nice rendition of flesh and bone. But, then, pure consciousness is a good basic description of anything.

All consciousness is imbued with the ability and desire to create; it's a family trait, so to speak, because that's exactly how All That Is is structured, and the progeny of All That Is carry the parent's trait. The legacy of creation cannot be used up, set aside or ignored. Creation happens, whether or not the consciousness involved acknowledges it and accepts its participation in the process.

The Spark of Creation

Mind, as we know it, is a tool bestowed on some individualized consciousness so it can explore ideas and constructs through new perceptions. Thought is the spark that ignites creation; without it, creation would halt. Take William James, for example. He is consciousness that, at present, has no physical appearance, yet he thinks, feels, desires and analyzes. If his ability to perceive had gone away upon physical death, he would literally be nonexistent, because the spark of creation would have died with him. (But since James is a part of All That Is, this is a moot point. No portion of All That Is can be annihilated; it can *look* like it no longer exists, but that's an illusion with no basis in truth.)

Thought and perception start the formation of overt physical symbols, whether those symbols become events or objects. And how is this little feat accomplished? James says that from his perspective there seems to be a malleable objective universe, or objective field, which consciousness molds to its liking when it wishes to experience form. The objective field is pliable and plastic. It's the medium upon which consciousness imprints its desires and intent, and then sits back and waits for actualization. Before form can be perceived, the thought, feeling or image of it must be projected outward from the mind onto the landscape of the objective field. The pattern of the inner desire of the consciousness involved in the creation of the object is then dutifully recognized and eventually brought into vivid existence.

So, the objective field, or what Seth calls Framework 2, is

not one that boasts of finished products and events. It encompasses the material that will eventually become the products and events, once consciousness decides exactly what it wants to create, and applies the mental stimuli to do so. According to James, "The objective field, then, is a medium with the propensity for leaning toward objectivity; it accepts mental stimuli which imprint it—stamp it—and form it into the habitual grooves of nature's shapes. It is manipulatable, gelatinlike, and composed of inclinations toward probable patterns upon which specifics ride."[9]

It seems that no matter where consciousness chooses to reside, the one given—the one law of the universe—is that it creates experience and form through thought, by using the "objective field"—and Seth, consciousness that he is, is no exception. "I have a fourteenth-century study, my favorite, with which I am very pleased...In your physical terms it does not exist, and I know quite well it is my mental production. Yet I enjoy it, and often take a physical form in order to sit at the desk and look out the window at the countryside.

"Now you do the same thing when you sit in your living room, but you do not realize what you are doing; and presently you are somewhat restricted. When my associates and I meet, we often translate each other's thoughts into various shapes and forms out of pure enjoyment in the practice."[10]

Consciousness comes first; matter follows. Some day our race will "get it;" then watch how fast the world changes.

Afterdeath Snapshots

But, meanwhile, we're still struggling with the idea of consciousness and what it means to life and death as we define them. On the surface we seem to have a grasp of physical life on earth; we seem well educated in all aspects of our existence. But what about after death? What do we really know of this state of being, and from where does our information come? For purposes of this discussion, we'll tip our hat to William James again and ask him for insights that can only come from the perspective of someone who has been there. The following is by no means the complete picture of experience after death, and it's not meant to be. It's simply a potpourri of snippets of information that draws a very intriguing picture of life after life as we know it.

When we're alive and well in physical reality, we hold an intense focus that heightens the vividness and clarity of life on earth. We perceive minute details, sharp corners, textured surfaces, brilliant colors. We see distance and space, brightness and dimness, movement and stillness. According to Seth, intense focus is a necessary maneuver by consciousness in physical form, because it keeps three-dimensionality "in place" and functioning, and blocks from our awareness other surrounding nonphysical activity that would only confuse our senses.

But what happens after we die? Our main focus has obviously altered radically—a good definition of death, by the way—but what now do we see, as far as physical reality is concerned? A dead William James compares what he views of our world with the negative of a photograph, "...unfleshed, showing outlines and definitions, but of a transparent nature. I have to 'read in' the perspectives that appear so realistically and colorfully to you, for my senses are not tuned in to those neurological keys that cause the world to spring alive."[11]

While definition of physical form blurs after death, it seems that *thought forms* take on more clarity and multidimensionality. For instance, James says that the events of his earth life, held as patterns of thought, now appear open-ended. He sees what occurred, but he also sees what he might have chosen to experience instead, and he sees how his life interacted with others' of which he was unaware. "Each contact, direct or not, counts and ripples outward so that each person's life sends out lines of contact intersecting with others on a psychic level...After death, watching the tracks of one's own influence is perhaps the most fascinating of endeavors...I could compare it to the tracking of a million lights simultaneously crisscrossing a night sky..."[12]

The dead can, if they choose, organize their thoughts along the same lines as when they were alive. However, few do, according to James, since this process is quite cumbersome and awkward. Instead, most newly dead quickly learn methods of accepting and integrating ideas with little delay. Usually all implications of the ideas are explored instantaneously in a multidimensional display of possibilities. No more waiting around for illumination, from the sound of it, unless the person chooses to block new insights—just as he or she might have while on earth.

The dead can also carry on discussions and conversations, just as in their earthly lifetimes, with one notable difference: Mental conversations are the mode of communication between nonphysical personalities, and these conversations take place when personalities seek each other out in friendship or through a desire to learn or share interests. James, for instance, hangs out with philosophers when he doesn't seek solitude, because his main propensity has always been, and it seems may always be, a love of philosophy. It seems obvious that the desire and intent of consciousness is the factor which selects the events it experiences, whether that consciousness resides on earth or elsewhere.

The ability to think doesn't end at death. If anything, it's heightened. Absorbing astonishing new ideas and delving into their meaning and implications, without the baggage of limiting beliefs established or accepted while alive in the three-dimensional world, is the purview of nonphysical consciousness. This is brought home to James when he senses the great learning process he's undergoing. He says, "Before my eyes flash again ages of more civilizations than I can count, each flourishing, using what seems to be the same planet in different fashions, each with different relationships between men and the other species, each reflecting these characteristics through their own languages and—oddest of all—interpreting man's state of being in completely different terms."[13] Soon James comprehends that this is a more accurate, more detailed picture of what occurs in actuality than man's belief in a one-past, one-history view of life.

The drama of learning continues after death, with great flourishes of vision and expanded methods of understanding. As Seth tells us, "There is no simple end to the life that you know, (such) as the story of heaven. There is the freedom to understand your own reality, to develop your abilities further, and to feel more deeply the nature of your own existence as a part of All That Is."[14]

Glimmers of Purpose and Meaning

Why do we care to know so many intimate details about consciousness? It's simple, really. By knowing the characteristics of consciousness, we can eventually understand how and why the universe functions as it does. When we know what drives consciousness, when we understand its communication system, and how and why it forms itself into certain structures, we can better understand ourselves and the purpose of physical life. And we just may—finally—become conscious creators of our existence, and conscious co-creators with the rest of the world.

It's time, you know.

2

All energy contains consciousness. That one sentence is <u>basically</u> scientific heresy, and in many circles, it is religious heresy as well. A recognition of that simple sentence would indeed change your world...
                                                           —*Seth*, The God of Jane, *Chapter 14*

Am I My Own Grandma?

Seth says, "...Energy cannot be considered without bringing to the forefront questions concerning the nature of God and All That Is, for the terms are synonymous."[1] This is certainly news to the classical sciences, which believe that consciousness is a by-product of materiality; that is, matter comes first and consciousness follows—if the right neurons and molecules are fortunate enough to join together and magically produce life. That consciousness is All That Is, that energy is consciousness, flies in the face of everything scientists have been taught to believe.

True, modern physics has proven that the thoughts of an observer alter physical events, that there is an interactive relationship between matter and consciousness, but many of the quantum physicists still drag their feet in accepting the implications of these findings. Why? Possibly because they would have to face the probability of God head on, and philosophy isn't their forte.

But the fact remains that until consciousness is seen as the force behind and within everything, our civilization will continue to base its assumptions and stances on erroneous conclusions. That's okay, no problem there—unless we're interested in minor issues like ending wars and eliminating diseases. Sooner or later, if we're smart, we'll step outside Newtonian, Darwinian and Freudian theories and broaden our mental and spiritual horizons. Major individual and world changes will come about because of it.

So, let's continue to delve into the subject of consciousness and see just exactly what the bigger picture brings to the party.

The Stuff of Life

First, it's crucial to understand that the outer world which we know so well actually emerges from an inner "psychological" world. That inner world is responsible for everything that happens in the outer world, and fuels it into existence. But it doesn't fuel it into existence on a wing and a prayer, or with blue smoke and mirrors. Behind everything—inner or outer—is the intelligence and logic of All That Is.

To better understand the basis of that intelligence and logic, we must first understand the tiniest dollop of consciousness, or what Seth calls consciousness units (CUs). These units are pure energy, the smallest possible unit of All That Is, coming into existence when All That Is created individualized consciousness. CUs are the building blocks of the universe, the stuff from which all else emerges. According to Seth, "Nothing exists—neither rock, mineral, plant, animal, or air—that is not filled with consciousness of its own kind...There is no object that was not formed by consciousness."[2] However, he cautions us that his discussion of the role of the CU in the creative process does not suggest that energy is divisible. It is, in fact, just the opposite. Energy cannot be divided into parts, ever. It is one; it is a continuum. But for purposes of learning, Seth defines basic components, or characteristics, of consciousness units. He says:

- They are a mental, nonphysical energy that is aware of itself.
- CUs exist outside time and space, move faster than light, and slow down to form matter.
- They are neither wave nor particle, but both.
- CUs are found in all places simultaneously, and are precognitive and clairvoyant.
- They weigh nothing and contain no mass.
- Each CU is imbued with great desire to fulfill itself through creativity.
- Each CU has the ability to organize, expand and develop along any lines it chooses.
- Free will allows a CU complete unpredictability, which supports the formation of infinite probabilities.
- CUs form themselves into groupings and systems of their choice, becoming their own camouflage and permeating that camouflage.

Consciousness units are pure energy, and that energy manifests itself as light. However, the light Seth talks about when discussing CUs isn't perceivable by us, it's not the usual garden variety of light that we see with our eyes. The light we take for granted is but a narrow bandwidth of the entire spectrum of light that exists beyond our perception. This "other" light is everywhere. So-called empty space is actually alive with consciousness units, or light. Indeed, there is no empty space in physical reality, not between pieces of furniture or between planets. The spaces are filled with the light that has its basis in CUs, the light that Seth says is the stuff "from which the very fires of life are lit," and which William James calls the "knowing light." It is, of course, the light of All That Is.

If everything is one light, how does consciousness differentiate itself into seemingly stand-alone structures? According to our cosmic friend Seth, consciousness uses electrically coded systems embedded within an overall electrical system. These code systems, infinite in number, hold different focuses. Each focus only allows certain data into its awareness, and what is allowed in is based on its significance to that particular code system. For instance, there are life forms that share the same light field with the life forms we intimately know (there is, after all, only one light field), but since the code system with which we are aligned doesn't choose to see these other life forms—and therefore ignores their code systems—their realities are effectively blocked from our awareness. This helps explain how everything in the universe exists in one "space" while seemingly in different places.

To add to this idea of an overall electrical system, here's Seth: "The electrical system possesses many dimensions of reality that cannot be perceived within the physical system...It is most difficult at this time to hint at the myriad complexity and dimension of the electrical actuality as it exists, when you consider that...experience is gathered together in particular ranges of intensities, again completely unique, codified; and this, the summation of all that you are, exists in one minute range or band of intensities."[3]

So, if Seth is correct about our universe being one big electrical system, why haven't our scientists discovered it?

Because the type of electricity Seth's talking about isn't your everyday household variety. He says, "...The electrical universe is composed of electricity that is far different from your idea of it. Electricity as you perceive it within the physical system is merely like an echo emanation, or sort of shadow image of these infinite varieties of pulsations...So far your scientists have only been able to study electricity by observing the projections of it that are perceivable within their frames of reference. As their physical instruments become more sophisticated, they will be able to glimpse more of this reality. But since they will not be able to explain it within their known system of references, many curious and distorted explanations of reported phenomena will be given."[4]

Going With the Flow

All consciousness is imbued with certain characteristics, as was noted at the beginning of this chapter. It is pure energy which has the power of creation within it and the free will to use that power as it chooses. Woven within itself is the ability and propensity not only to create any form of matter and any universe, but to become a part of its creations.

Now, a really interesting thing about consciousness is that it's never formed into a structure and told to stay that way by All That Is. Because it has free will, it can move around here and there, trying on this form and that one, mixing with other consciousnesses and creating new forms if it wishes. It can become part of a large organization, scale itself down into a more simple construct, or be a part of both simultaneously. It can send part of itself into a form just for fun and send another portion of itself somewhere else at the same time—never losing its oneness or overall identity. And when it's ready to move on, it does, with other consciousness filling in the resultant gap, if appropriate.

What this flexibility of consciousness boils down to is that no system that is created by it—no reality, no physical or nonphysical form, no universe—is a closed system. That is, consciousness energy can and does flow into or out of anything at will, either a portion at a time or *en masse*. For instance, consciousness may choose to withdraw completely from a physical body (called death in our terms), or perhaps send part of its physical energy into the formation of a tree ...while still maintaining the physical body.

Because of this potential of movement, you can see that consciousness is very fluid. Picture it as a congruent field of CUs, seemingly individual but actually one, swarming to become universes and planets and people and animals and driftwood and space and mountains and nails, and then expanding into new formations or moving on to create other structures, when desired. And if a mountain still wishes to "be" after a portion of its consciousness pulls out, another bit of consciousness will join the mountain and keep it in place.

With all this freewheeling allowed and encouraged of consciousness, how can the universe possibly run smoothly?

The Grander Design

This is where it gets dicey. Not the reality of the situation, but the explanation of it. The last thing Seth wants us to do is assign levels and hierarchies to consciousness—concepts that suggest an *evolution* of spirituality is necessary to reach the next threshold. The problem is that this is what we've been taught by our religions, theologies and spiritual teachings through the centuries, this idea of aspiring to the next higher, distinct level of growth...usually through hard work and/or mental self-flagellation. Because of our entrenched beliefs about the truths of such concepts, we sometimes find it difficult set them aside, if we care to question them at all.

But that line of thinking is exceedingly limiting when dealing with the subject of consciousness. By holding on to such ideas, we mentally condense the magnificence and power of the reality of which we are a part to a mere shadow of its former self; a shadow that vibrates with the belief that physical reality is low on the totem pole of spiritual evolution. The unfortunate result is that we get scaled down right along with the belief, and our magnificence and power seem nowhere to be found.

So, while we're about to discuss distinctions between human consciousness and the greater consciousness that creates it, just remember there *aren't* any distinctions. Through experience and knowledge, consciousness develops different awareness levels, none more sacrosanct or spiritual than the other. They're simply expressions of the consciousness of All That Is—and All That Is is already spiritual.

With that disclaimer posted and noted, let's start with the definition of a consciousness gestalt, from which everything unfolds. You won't find the phrase "consciousness gestalt" in *Webster's*, but there is a definition of gestalt. It is "…a structure, configuration, or pattern of physical, biological, or psychological phenomena so integrated as to constitute a functional unit with properties not derivable from its parts in summation." If we add the word psychic (i.e. "…psychic, physical, biological, or psychological phenomena"), we define a consciousness gestalt.

Expanded upon, a consciousness gestalt is a psychological grouping of consciousness units that have come together with purpose and intent. The grouping is a part of All That Is that wishes to explore certain creative ventures. The CUs are drawn to each other through the propensity of their nature; that is, they have tendencies of similar strength and focus.

Each human being is a consciousness gestalt which has been created by a much larger consciousness gestalt, then sent on its way to form experiences and feed them into the whole for interpretation. The same also applies to the various larger consciousness gestalts that formed each of us. In other words, there are other, larger gestalts that formed them and sent them on their way to form experiences, etc., etc. This goes on ad infinitum up and down the line, and the whole-plus is called All That Is.

Other than our self, we usually want to know the most about the consciousness gestalt that is directly responsible for our personal existence. Seth and Jane call it by various names, such as whole self, source self, soul, larger psychological self, entity and greater self. We'll use greater self for the purpose of this discussion.

A greater self is an enormous psychological energy gestalt which produces not only countless smaller gestalts, but the realities in which they reside. A greater self's creations may show up in physical reality, and some may appear in other realities very foreign to our way of thinking. But always, without exception, the smaller energy gestalts, or personalities, are never cut off from their creator. They remain very much a part of it, with only the illusion of separateness.

Those personalities created by a greater self and inserted into physical reality are spread throughout the centuries, playing the roles their beliefs and historical time frames suggest are appropriate. For instance, one greater self might have a serf in ancient Mesopotamia, a housewife in present-day Mexico, a king in fifteenth-century England. It might also have hundreds or thousands of other personalities concurrently acting out their roles in other times and places. Since time and space are only created for and used in physical reality, a greater self ignores them. It scatters its personalities hither and yon throughout linear time, and keeps watch over them all—simultaneously. It sees the Mexican housewife turn on the television set and view the evening news, all the while keeping tabs on the English king busily planning for his kingdom's fall harvest, and the Mesopotamian serf cooking his morning gruel.

A greater self doesn't just place personalities into different space/time contexts throughout history. It can, and does, place many into identical or overlapping time frames. In other words, your next-door neighbor, or Saddam Hussein, or a black ghetto child may be of the same greater self as you. What you learn, what comprehensions and knowledge are gathered during your lifetime, are funneled into your greater self, along with the learnings of its other personalities, however far-flung they seem to be in time and space, and different in world views.

Uniquely Yours

Counterparts are what Seth calls those people alive in the same time context who originate from the same greater self. In the example above, for instance, you, your next-door neighbor, Saddam Hussein and the black ghetto child would be counterparts. The larger psychological entity of which you are a part would manifest not just one person in a given time period, but many. Here's how Seth describes it: "...When your 'original self' enters (part of) itself into three-dimensional life from an inner reality, the energy waves carrying it break—not simply into one particle...but into a number of conscious particles...They spread out from the 'point of contact,' forming individual lives...There are other counterparts of yourself living at the same time and in different places—all creative versions of the original self."[5]

Counterparts come from the same "psychic pool," but physically they can be as different as night and day. They assume a variety of ages, nationalities, sexual orientations, family roles, etc., because in this way the abilities and propensities of the greater self can be given wider range. Also, from these very different viewpoints the greater self gathers to it insights that just one expression of itself in physicality might not experience.

Counterparts may or may not meet in their joint lifetime, depending on circumstances and needs, but meet they do in other ways. Psychically they are always in touch, at times so much so that they read each other's thoughts. In the dream state they come together, playing roles for each other that echo the lessons they've individually learned—in essence, trying to help each other get on with the most fulfilling life possible. When they do meet in the "real" world, and if they pair up as a couple or in another type of relationship, they are usually merging for common purposes and goals. While their approach to life may seem at odds at times, they may simply be exploring different ways of solving the same kind of challenge.

Time-Seeding Our Selves

And what of those personalities salted throughout the centuries by your greater self, the ones not living in today's world, but very much alive at the same time as you, yet in their own historical periods? Some of them are *you* in other forms.

The belief in reincarnation has been around for a long time. Its usual definition is one that portrays a soul on a journey through linear time, experiencing the diversity of life, paying the price for failures and nastiness and reaping rewards for goodness and love in its next existence, and finally growing wise enough to achieve the ultimate...spiritual perfection. Then it's time to blow this popsicle joint, never having to return to such a lowly creature-based reality. Graduation happens.

But Seth says we've got most of it wrong. We can't be any more spiritual than we already are. We can be more *aware* of our natural state of spirituality and act accordingly, but by virtue of our cosmic heritage (i.e., as a part of All That Is), we're there. And our "growth" takes on a different hue when viewed through the lens of nonlinear time. It's true we usually lead many lives on earth, but we're leading them all right now. So how can our actions in one life lead to specific repercussions in the "next" one? Seth says, "...What you understand of reincarnation, and of the time terms involved, is a very simplified tale indeed...Reincarnation, in its own way, is also a parable. It seems very difficult for you to understand that you live in many realities—and many centuries—at one time..."[6]

Since there is no linear time in the greater scheme of things, all events, all experiences are occurring at once. In order to hold our focus in physical reality, we block from our awareness the other times and places surrounding us, and pretend there is only one reality happening at a time... and ours is it. But Seth says, "At the same 'time,' so to speak, that this personality is born into a minority race, in a completely different era it may be born rich, secure and aristocratic. It is searching out different methods of experience and expansion."[7] The full self of which we are a part is multitudinous, not singular, and it is dead set on expressing itself in limitless ways through limitless time.

The fascinating thing about each of us living all our lives simultaneously is that we communicate with our other selves on a regular basis. According to Seth, some of our inspiration and insight comes from others of "us" who have inputs to share, and these inputs come to us in our dreams or waking state. The sudden answer to a current problem, the strength just when we need it, the optimism that seemed lacking yesterday but floods today sometimes comes from other portions of our self who are experiencing those issues. And vice versa from us to them. It seems those of us who are "assigned" to physical reality by our greater selves share a special bond, and we keep in touch psychically, ignoring the boundaries of time and space.

Each personality of ours, each self who we are in another time and place, is exploring physical reality through the very fine focus of its personal present, just as we are, and each of us is always uniquely individual. Our greater self "does not simply send out an old self in new clothes time and time again, but each time sends a new, freshly-minted self that then develops and goes its own way."[8] Yet on another level we are part of a very interesting whole, one that works in concert to assimilate its diverse learnings into a package of knowledge and insight available to all of its parts for their personal growth and understanding. We truly are one. As our friend Seth says, "Since all lives are simultaneous, all happening at once, then any separation is a psychological one."[9]

Psychic Offshoots

As though there weren't enough physical expressions of our selves romping through the centuries as reincarnational aspects and counterparts, the universe is seeded with another type of multidimensional "us." This one is called a probable self.

First, a review. Consciousness is composed of pure energy. Our greater selves are conglomerations of highly charged energy. We, in turn, and all our reincarnational and counterpart selves, are smaller configurations of the same energy. We were brought into being when our greater selves formed patterns of energy they wished to actualize into specific physical forms (never mind for now all the nonphysical patterns they also actualize, right along with the physical ones—greater selves are very productive).

Each of the physical forms created by our source energy can be considered a nucleus of consciousness. Seth says that that nucleus, according to its intensity, will attract to it certain discrete energy patterns that have the possibility of developing into full-blown, alternate physical manifestations of itself. What that means in plain English is that when we are born we are surrounded by a variety of probable selves we may choose to become as time moves on. Each of those selves also is its own nucleus in the same situation... i.e., it is surrounded by *its* probable selves.

So, at birth we surround ourselves with possible variations of our personhood, and as we progress through life we can draw from this bank of possible forms the ones we wish to become. As we make choices after birth as to what we'll believe and who we want to become, we may align our present self so strongly with a probable self that that probable self either merges with our present self, bringing with it its distinct qualities, or the probable self becomes the main focus of energy in this lifetime.

Seth, in explaining the concept to Rob Butts, used Rob's life as an example: "Your 'sportsman self' was never endowed with the same kind of force as that of your artistic or writing self. It became subsidiary, yet present to be drawn upon, taking joy through your motion and adding its vitality to your 'main' personality. Had it been given extra force through your environment, circumstances, or your own intent, then either your artistic self would have become subservient or complementary; or, if the energy selves were of nearly equal intensity, then one of them would have become an offshoot, propelled by its own need for fulfillment into a probable reality."[10]

Because no energy systems are closed, energy flows freely between them—and any consciousness gestalt is an energy system. All portions of a greater self's creations communicate and interact as energy moves between them. Probable selves, just like counterparts and reincarnational selves, unconsciously know of their interrelationships. They work together to fulfill the intent of the original nucleus. Seth describes some of the decisions made thusly: "An offshoot probable self might leave your reality at age 13, say, but could intersect with you again at age 30 for a variety of reasons—where to you, you suddenly change a profession, or become aware of a talent you thought you had forgotten, and find yourself developing it with amazing ease."[11]

The deal is that any consciousness will always try to express itself in all of its probable directions. If you don't choose to become a certain probable self in this lifetime, then that probable self has the right, the propensity to enter another reality where it can become the main character, so to speak. And if it, in turn, doesn't choose to become a certain probable self that is available to it in that new reality, the probable self not chosen has the right, the propensity to...well, you get the idea.

Seth Multiplied

How do reincarnational selves, counterparts and probable selves tie together? The price we pay for language that cannot contain concepts so immense as the creativity of consciousness is that we must package and label the whole into parts that seem divided. But, as we said earlier, there are no distinctions.

Seth says he uses terms like reincarnation and counterparts to preserve our sense of identity, which we're so afraid of losing. It sounds to me as though Seth feels these words bring us comfort, because we can intellectually discuss the enormity of the consciousness of which we are a part and try to make sense of where we fit into the picture. But at times something seems lost in the translation. We start to perceive divisions...us and them, my historical time and their historical time, my reality and their reality, offshoots and primary, a greater self and little ol' me. But it's really all one consciousness.

One evening just before Jane started speaking as Seth for their twice-weekly book dictation sessions, she found herself entering an altered state of consciousness unlike her usual one. She saw many different images of Seth, large and small, intertwined, moving and somewhat stylized. When Seth finally came through for their session, he explained what Jane had experienced. He said she had seen images of him in a way that would help her more clearly understand the limitless nature of the psyche.

Basically, the information she received conveyed the idea that no one identity can be developed or expressed simply by assuming one form. Of the "Seths" Jane saw, Seth said: "Each one is involved in its own context of reality, each one pursuing its own directions for its own purposes. One of those 'Seths' was born in your space and time. That Seth then seeded himself, so to speak, in the space-time environment you recognize—appearing through the centuries, sending out offshoots of 'himself,' exploring earthly experience and developing as well as he could those potentials of his own greater identity that could best be brought to fruition within a creature context. That one Seth was endowed with his own inner blueprint. The blueprint gave him an idea of his potentials, and how they could best be fulfilled in earthly terms."[12]

This statement by Seth tells us so very much. Not only are we not "less" by splitting off and becoming other aspects of ourselves, we are magnified. Call them counterparts, probable selves, reincarnational selves or whatever you choose—the bottom line is it's one psyche exploring its potential in as many ways as possible, following the inner blueprint of its intent.

That said, however, it seems important to note that while we are part of a whole, we are nonetheless uniquely individual. Seth says we each have an indestructible validity that is sacredly inviolate. And, since the universe does not run on fluff, we can assume it has the means of keeping our unique personality separate from the rest of our soul's manifestations.

Indeed it does.

Our individuality starts when we are sparked into being by our inner self. And from then on, every effect we experience is recorded as a series of electrical signals and codes that form an electrical pattern. The electrical pattern exists independently of physical reality, but is also found within it. In fact, the cells of our bodies form *around* the electrical pattern, and change as the pattern changes.

So, as we experience more and more of physical life, the effects of those experiences are coded electrically and added to our electrical pattern. Then, the cells of our bodies change to accommodate the new data found in that pattern, and in essence create a physical counterpart to the nonphysical pattern. Both patterns, or more accurately, the one pattern echoed both within and outside time and space, becomes the complete picture of our experience and our personality. Upon death all we do is drop the physical casing that surrounds the electrical pattern—and then go on to integrate our pattern into that of our greater self. We, in essence, change from physical reality fully into electrical reality.

Families of a Different Stuff

Purpose and meaning run rampant in our lives...indeed, in the universe. Everything we've discussed so far clearly suggests and supports that statement. How much more can be said that will prove to us that there is great intent behind why we're here and how we set the stage for the further development of our consciousness? Plenty, actually, but we'll focus for now on something called families of consciousness.

As Seth tells us again and again, we are individually unique. Our individuality comes before anything else, no matter in what state of being we find ourselves. We adopt a certain set of unique characteristics for our own reasons, and then we set about developing our multiple lives based on the growth potential inherent in those characteristics.

Consciousness likes organization, and it tends to be drawn to others who hold similar inner traits. Groupings form based on an overall outlook toward life. Seth calls these groupings families of consciousness or psychic families. He says we have an inner affiliation with a unique kind of consciousness that "makes use of certain boundaries." These inner affiliations lead us to join psychic families whose members generally hold in common characteristics that loosely bind them as a group, just as a human family or members of countries might hold characteristics in common. Seth seems to stress this point, so I will also: We join psychic families because we share an overall viewpoint of reality. Our interests and abilities come before our entry into such a grouping, however, and are not predetermined by our membership in a given family of consciousness.

Seth names nine psychic families in *The "Unknown" Reality, Volume 2*, and describes their various characteristics, emphasizing how the attributes of the whole combine to form civilization. To state the obvious, no one family is superior to another, and all have their roles to play in the development of life on earth. The members of the families are spread across nationalities and sprinkled throughout social and economic groups. During different historical periods, some families tend to predominate the world scene; but, according to Seth, families almost always "operate as systems of creative checks and balances" for each other.

All psychic families share traits, or, said differently, traces of all traits can be found in all families and all personalities within those families. Some traits may be more predominant in one family than another, however. For instance, Jane, Rob, and many of the people who attended Jane's ESP classes held over many years were of the Sumari family. Of Sumari, Seth says they generally are creatively playful, very independent, practical, self-reliant, given to art, not given to belonging to a structured group, not fighters, and seldom conformers. Picasso, he says, was a Sumari.

Choosing our psychic family is based on what we like. Says friend Seth, "You like to be an initiator or a follower or a nourisher. You like to create variations on old systems, or you like to create new ones. You like to deal primarily with healing, or with information, or with physical data. You like to deal with sight, or sound, with dreams, or with translating inner data into the working psychic material of your society. So you choose a certain focus, as you choose ahead of time your physical family."[13]

Are counterparts of the same psychic family? More often than not. According to Seth, "There is a connection between counterparts and the families of consciousness. As your brothers and sisters might belong to the same physical family, so generally are you and your counterparts part of the same psychic group of consciousness."[14]

Consciousness always has free will. If it chooses to change families, it has the ability to do so. Further, new families and subfamilies form when circumstances deem appropriate. Just as the human races mix, so do psychic families. Consciousness can and does mingle and interrelate at will with other consciousnesses, and once in a while a new family will form from the new sub-groupings.

Complicated? According to Seth, "A book would be needed to explain the dimensions of the psyche in relation to the different families of consciousness. Here...I merely want to make the reader aware of the existence of these psychic groupings. I am alert to the fact that I am using many terms, and that it may seem difficult to understand the differences between probable and reincarnational selves, counterparts and families of consciousness. At times contradictions may seem to exist. You may wonder how you are you in the midst of such multitudinous psychic 'variations.'"[15]

Well, shoot, I never wondered about it. Did you?

And the Beat Goes On

Obviously there is no predetermination as to who we will become and what we will do with our life. Flexibility is the key: the flexibility of consciousness to make free-will choices as it tests the waters of time and space. And when it's had enough of physical life, either forever or for awhile, it withdraws its energy from this reality and heads on home to spend time with its source self. Then, after a refreshing interlude, if that's what it chooses to experience, what consciousness does with its life is again its choice. Physical reality is always an option, but so are other realities, depending on what it wants to experience and what it has chosen as its next path of development.

One thing is abundantly clear, though: Life is neither a progression from birth to lasting death, nor a journey through linear time of many bodies in successive order. The setting aside of both theories is perhaps one of the most freeing moves we can make, because once we do we've cleared the way for new ideas and knowledge that previously had nowhere to go except full force into the solid wall of our old beliefs. And where there is no give, there is no room for new insights.

For instance, if we know we live more than one life, that we're eternally multidimensional, perhaps we can assume we're not sinful creatures here for a one-time shot at Heaven, or a one-time assignment to Hell. And if we live all our lives simultaneously and share those lives with counterparts and probable selves, perhaps we can assume we're not here to "grow" into our spirituality, with hell to pay in the next life if we screw up this one. Perhaps we can stop using fear as the impetus to be good, solid, kind people and use, instead, the knowledge of our origins in consciousness, our literal oneness with each other and All That Is, to help us understand why, if we hurt even one person, we ultimately hurt ourselves. Perhaps if we really, truly change our beliefs about who we are, where we come from and where we're going, we'll have no need to fear ourselves or others. The pieces of life's puzzle will fall into place, and we'll see that, as we said before, purpose and meaning run rampant in our existence.

The Road Ignored

And how does most of science cope with this expanded picture of reality which stresses the all-inclusivity of consciousness? Not at all, basically. The majority of scientists don't cope at all, because they choose not to step outside the quantifiable stuff of physical reality. And it is a choice. If scientists were willing to explore the quote of Seth's that says "All energy contains consciousness," it would mean they had taken the first step in allowing for its possibility. But that presents a quandary. Scientists would then have to study the enormous implications of the statement. And when the implications became apparent, the scientists would be forced to reassess their present theories and conclusions. A massive upheaval would ensue, the likes of which the world hasn't seen since Sir Isaac Newton defined a mechanistic world of classical cause and effect.

Most of the men and women of science wear blinders that effectively block from their understanding what common sense and intuition surely must at some time reflect to them: The universe is with meaning and purpose. Of himself, William James says after death: "My own (physical) existence gave me evidence of the soul's existence: I knew it but dismissed this as beside the point since in no way could I produce the scientific proof that—alone, I felt—could demonstrate to others the actuality of such a hypothesis. As scientific technique, that was proper. But as a man I pretended not to know what I knew but could not prove before my fellows."[16]

And therein lies the glitch: Consciousness cannot be proven, using scientific methods and technologies. Consciousness is not a quantum particle to be analyzed through mathematical equations and scientific instrumentation. Consciousness creates the minds of the people who design the equations and it creates the instruments they use. Yet at the same time it is outside the minds and instruments. Consciousness will never be isolated in a laboratory, because it creates the laboratory and the scientists who work therein. It becomes its own camouflage, pretending to be matter and forces and people.

If individual scientists acknowledge consciousness at all, most of the time they see it as distinctly separate from matter. They might even postulate the question, When does consciousness enter matter to form life? That matter and consciousness are inseparable, indeed identical, seems to be too far removed from their present theories to accept. However, while atoms, molecules and subatomic particles can be identified, they are not the end all. The end all resides outside time and space, and creates the quantum stuff and the nonquantum stuff—and determines how it all works together.

What science sees and measures is only the tip of the iceberg of physical reality, what seems predictable, and, as such, hard fact. But as universal physicist Seth says, "Science likes to think that it deals with predictable action. It perceives such a small amount of data, however, and in such a limited area, that the great inner underpredictability of any molecule, atom, or wave is not apparent. Scientists perceive only what appears within your system, and that often appears predictable."[17]

To study consciousness demands we mothball our penchant for measuring devices and measurable tests. It means we explore consciousness with our minds and through our feelings, that we follow its trail through our intuition and dreams and the symbolism of the events we encounter in life—that, in essence, we go within to understand the world outside. William James says, "...Science since my time has compromised itself, and while it was once the harbor of the truth seeker who escaped religion's dictates and dogma, now the truth seeker must steadfastly stand apart from science and religion alike."[18] Perhaps we shouldn't be too quick to divorce ourselves from the bright minds of our scientists, but for the good of all they will eventually need to open their boundaries and contemplate the existence of an inner world that can be explored just as surely as the outer one they know so well.

And when that happens their inner explorations will lead to an entirely new science, one brought into being by a deeper philosophy of understanding. The new science can't come first; it must be preceded by a body of thought that leaves signposts which the scientists can use to map the emerging discipline. Without a new body of thought to study and explore, the scientists will never form the questions that will lead to major breakthroughs in their specialties—because they will never see beyond the obvious.

Scientists acknowledge that energy and matter are one.

Now it's time to recognize that energy and matter and consciousness are one.

3

It was only after death that I understood life's full achievement; appreciated the fine focus of consciousness tuned so precisely and triumphantly to one place and time; and felt the power of earth-dimensioned life as in life I had never known it. As a result I came to terms with my own spirit, and gave it its freedom while in life I overtended it, believing that it was ill served by mortality's experience.

—William James, The Afterdeath Journal of an
American Philosopher, *Chapter 2*

Consciousness in Physical Attire

The unfortunate part about our placing such trust and belief in today's masters of science and the merchants of theology is that neither discipline offers the individual a sense of unqualified personal, eternal validity and integrity. We're characterized more as flash-in-the-pan bodies with a truck load of errors, omissions and failures dragging us down. The more I understand who we really are, the more absurd it seems that we allow ourselves to believe such nonsense at all, let alone help perpetuate it by our staunch support and acceptance of it. We are incredible people living in an incredible world. That most of us don't realize it is indicative of just how far we've removed ourselves from inner knowledge that exists in our very cells and psyche, and it's indicative of the events we experience because we misunderstand,

and therefore unknowingly misuse, the power at our finger-tips.

It's time we began thinking for ourselves, asking questions we've never before dreamed of, searching for answers in all the "wrong" places, and then making up our own minds as to the value of this new/old information. Hey, what have we got to lose?

What have we got to gain? How about a sense of identity and purpose that brings excitement back into our existence, that gives us a new lease on life? How about knowledge that suggests how to become successful and loved and abundant? How about an inner knowing that tells us the world is our oyster, full of pearls for the asking—the pearls being of our own choice and definition?

Let's take a further look at consciousness, then, because that's where the knowledge that frees us resides. In the last two chapters we talked about consciousness in general and how it seeds the universe and physical reality in a myriad of ways. Now we'll focus on the specifics of consciousness in human form.

Cosmic Beginnings

Most of the world's problems stem from the fact that the majority of its population has no sense of itself in greater form, no deep-seated feelings of connectedness with anything other than its ego. The physical eyes reveal a world that looks worse for the wear most of the time, without solace or serenity. Feeling cut off from everything and every being, physically and spiritually, seems to be a mass condition. If consciousness is with purpose and intent, and if consciousness forms its reality, there seems to be a piece of life's puzzle that's not apparent or accepted by most of today's people. What might that puzzle piece be?

As it turns out, the puzzle piece is singular but appears

plural. It's a puzzle piece that speaks of multidimensionality and inner and outer worlds, of psychic bridges between seemingly disparate portions of the self. It's a puzzle piece with all the answers to expanded and fulfilling lives, because it opens our minds to thrilling probabilities we never dreamed possible. And it starts with the inner self.

Each person has an inner self which created him or her. The inner self is a portion of the person's greater self assigned the task of not only forming him or her in physical reality, but creating his or her physical reality as well. Each of us remains a part of our inner self after birth, so much so that it not only sustains life in our body, but regulates it according to our expressed wishes. Our inner self also extends itself into our reality through our conscious mind, and *as* our conscious mind. As Seth says, "Your inner self adopts the physically conscious, physically focused mind as a method of allowing it to manipulate in the world that you know. The conscious mind is particularly equipped to direct outward activity, to handle waking experience and oversee physical work."[1]

Then there is the ego, the part of us that is most obvious, the part that is formed from a group of characteristics originally selected by the inner self and modified over time by beliefs and life's experiences. The ego is the focus through which the conscious mind views physical reality, the part that monitors the information that flows into the mind. It sits atop the conscious mind, if you will, picking and choosing what it wants to accept as valid input, and discarding the rest as irrelevant to its belief system. The cast-off information is then assigned storage in the subconscious, useable whenever the ego changes its outlook on life enough to allow it to resurface as pertinent data.

The subconscious is not a chilling cave of irrational desires and aggressive impulses, or a haven of goodness and light. As Jane Roberts says in *How To Develop Your ESP Power*, "It is a storehouse for all the impressions and abilities not accepted by the ego at any given time. It is the threshold between the so-called conscious self, and those vast inner areas of the self..." The subconscious is the gateway to the multidimensional self; in other words, the layer of the mind found between the conscious mind and the greater portions of the whole self.

So the complete person evolves from and is part of the inner self, which creates a body, a conscious mind, an ego and a subconscious mind as the package of who we are, and then creates our reality in the likeness of our conscious desires, intents and beliefs. There is no delineation between the parts, for they flow smoothly into one whole. However, each part has a role to play that is individual, and all are crucial to the development of the human being. When working in harmony, they emerge as the missing puzzle piece. When working in harmony, they create the stuff of dreams...a fulfilling life.

Running Scared

Why, then, don't we all create fulfilling lives as a matter of course? We have the obvious potential to do just that, so why do our private lives seem in disarray much of the time? Illnesses, lacks, angers, attacks—why do we allow such disharmony to penetrate our creations? The finger of judgment points to the ego, but the poor thing doesn't deserve the rap. Well, in some ways it does, but only because of its lack of understanding its role in the bigger picture.

The ego is an expert in its field. It's trained to deal directly with the contents of the conscious mind, and its focus is on the material portions of our existence. It firmly focuses itself outward into physicality, with the responsibility to gauge what's happening and feed that data back into the conscious mind—which, because it is used by the inner self to monitor the exterior world which it created, has an easy time of transferring that data into the metaphoric hands of the inner self for processing.

So, the inner self receives the interpretation of the experiences of the physical self from the ego via the conscious mind. It doesn't pass judgment on the ego's interpretations; it simply takes that raw data and creates what the ego expects to see, because the job of the inner self it to build our realities based on what we tell it to do through our thoughts.

And here is where our physical creations can fall apart rather quickly. The conscious mind is meant to make clear judgments about what is happening in our life and our reality. Unfounded beliefs held by the ego color what the conscious mind sees and clouds its vision. When the ego feels cut off, lonely, afraid, it runs all over the more balanced views of the conscious mind. The ego starts to believe there is no link to an inner self, that *it* is the beginning and end of a human's self, that when the body dies, it's all over. The ego builds itself into a mini-god and quakes in its boots because it bases its godhood on what it sees—and what it sees is based on its past eyesight, which was based on its fears. All of a sudden the ego is completely vulnerable, or so it believes.

The conscious mind, which knows better, takes a back seat to the ego, not because the ego is more powerful, but because the inner self set it up that way. The ego's responsibilities are to regulate what goes to the conscious mind as perceptions of reality and to stay balanced. But if it doesn't, the rest of the self goes along with the ego's interpretation of it all, and lets it run where it will...which usually means into the walls of hurt and problems.

How did so many of our collective egos run amok for so many centuries? According to Seth, they became so enamored of the exterior world they "forgot" there was an inner one, and in so doing, forgot their heritage and how that heritage forms the outer world. What happened next is what must be rectified before our race will meet its potential: The ego became very afraid. It started to feel lonely, insignificant, lost to the whole, part of nothing. And because of the unique way the universe functions, the personality started meeting the ego's feelings as situations and life experiences. The ego felt a threat to its survival and fought against it, initiating unnecessary struggles. From the ego's disassociation came what is now standard operating procedure in this reality... wars, hatred, bigotry, isolation, hardships, illnesses, sadness, depression, desperation...the list seems to never end.

A Helping Hand

The solution to all our troubles starts with this: The ego must come to see itself as the most exterior portion of the inner self, not cut off or alienated, but an integral part of the inner self looking outward into physicality. It needs to see its "I" as far greater than itself. And it's got to stop running around like a chicken with its head cut off, frantically trying to make sense of exterior data only, and completely ignoring the suggestions and directions being fed to it all the time by the deeper portions of itself. Seth says, "You have allowed the ego to become a counterfeit self, and you take its word because you will not hear the muffled voice that is within it."[2] What's this muffled voice? Obviously it's the voice of the inner self, and it turns out to be the ego's savior.

Throughout recorded history, humankind has searched for psychic maps leading to inner assistance and knowledge, knowledge that can't be discovered through reason. And yet the maps have always been there, imbedded in the very fabric of our psyches, somehow hidden by our sense of powerlessness and insignificance. Such information is available to

each of us, however, and from it springs the path to the fulfillment of our individual aspirations and the dreams of our
race.

The ego is meant to receive and accept this data from the
inner self. It's part of the ego's job, so to speak, part of what it
signed up to do when it became an intrinsic piece of the human personality. But when the ego holds a limited conception of reality, when it becomes overbearing and fearful, it
becomes rigid. This rigidity, in turn, leads to more anxiety,
because the ego is forced to deal with life from a position of
limited knowledge. The anxiety then reinforces the ego's belief that it must try to control all aspects of life, because there
is no other input it feels it can rely on.

But there is. Seth says, "In normal living and in day-by-
day experience, all the knowledge you need is available. You
must, however, <u>believe</u> that it is, put yourself in a position to
receive it by looking inward and remaining open to your
intuitions, and most important, by <u>desiring</u> to receive it."[3]
Slowly, the ego can be taught to loosen its hold enough to
allow inner information to surface without automatic dis-
missal. The inner logic that forms the inner information can
then be seen as being just as important as the outer logic
controlled by the ego, instead of out-of-control, chaotic, broken bits of non-logic arising from the dark subconscious.

The inner self would like that. It's been waiting around
for centuries for the return of the ego to the fold. There's so
much it wants to tell that errant part of the whole, so much
that will bring comfort and excitement and new direction to
the lost portion of the soul. Some of what the inner self
wants to say is lighten up. And learn. Because there's so
much you don't yet know, but obviously need to, and it can
be fun.

So, ego, listen up and we'll fill in some of the blanks.

Our Gift of Life

It seems important that we truly understand the inner self, at least as much as is possible while represented in physical form, because the reason for our being is delicately intertwined with the reason for its being. Perhaps if we understand the inner self more fully, we will grasp the intimacy we share with it and what it means to the natural development of our lives.

First of all, the inner self is highly conscious of itself, just as we are (somewhat) conscious of ourselves. In other words, it's not simply an energy field that accepts input, massages the data and spits out an event or material object. It *knows* itself. It is a thinking, action-oriented energy gestalt with tremendous power at its fingertips and the high intelligence to use it. It has to be pretty smart, if you think about it, to use its massive knowledge and unlimited scope of consciousness to form the physical world, not just once but on a moment-by-moment basis, over and over again, ad infinitum, in concert with all other inner selves.

According to our cosmic expert Seth, our inner selves chose physical reality as a dimension in which they would express themselves; they chose to embark upon the exciting undertaking of learning how to translate *their* realities into physical terms. So, they had to know how to "form and maintain the physical basis upon which all else must depend—the properties of earth that can be called natural ones."[4] This suggests our inner selves have a vast reservoir of knowledge from which to draw, and Seth backs up that assumption: "There is, after the operating ego, a layer of personal subconscious material. Beneath this is racial material dealing with the species as a whole. Beneath this, undistorted and yours for the asking, is the knowledge inherent in the inner self, pertaining to reality as a whole, its laws, principles, and composition.

"Here you will find the innate knowledge concerning the creation of the camouflage universe as you know it, the mechanics involved, and much of the material I have given you. You will find the ways and means by which the inner self, existing in the climate of psychological reality, helps create the various planes of existence, constructs outer senses to project and perceive these, and the ways by which reincarnations take place within various systems. Here you will find your own answers as to how the inner self transforms energy for its own purposes, changes its form, and adopts other realities."[5]

Here's the situation. For their own growth, our combined inner selves decided to create a medium called physical reality. They agreed upon the details and root assumptions of the reality they were about to form, and decided what knowledge they would need to pull it off. That knowledge then became accessible to them, so they proceeded with the plan. Part of the plan, of course, included creating personalities that could function in a physical reality, not only as human beings, but as thinking beings. So, bodies, conscious minds, egos and subconscious minds—all direct extensions of the energy of the inner selves, formed from their ideas— were created by them and remain a part of them. In essence, our inner selves honed a way to experience physical reality, and that way included experiencing it through the expressions of each of us.

In order to keep things interesting and unpredictable— keep the excitement of their learning knife-edge sharp, as it were—our inner selves endowed us with the free will to choose the events of our lives from infinite possibilities. Our free will would keep our inner selves on their toes, you see, because they would never be able to predict for sure what we would choose to experience. But free will would need checks and balances, at times, such as when we seem to veer too far from our purpose and find ourselves divorced from the inner knowledge of our source—i.e., in deep trouble.

At times like that, the inner self will buoy us with its support. It will still create our distorted truths for us to see, because that's its job, but it will also form its deeper, clearer truths into physically-oriented data that will show up in our life. Just when we hit rock bottom, we meet a friend of a friend who loans us a book—and we cry at the impact it has on us and our immediate needs. When we think we can draw no solace from an emotionally-torn world, an animal protects a little boy from grave danger, and it makes the evening news. Seeing truths like these projected into physicality helps the ego accept another version of reality different from the one it had begun to hold dear.

On a more direct level, when our inner self is alerted to the danger of a budding event we're creating, whatever it may be (an accident in the making, for instance), Seth says it will "immediately try to remedy the situation by an influx of self-corrective measures. On occasion, when the situation gets out of hand, (the inner self) will bypass those restrictive areas of the conscious mind, and solve the problem by shooting forth energy in other layers of activity."[6] That is, of course, if we don't throw an emotional fit and demand to have our way through the rigidity of our limiting beliefs and intent.

And on a grander scale, our combined inner selves will craft symbols and events that will most impact the world's population when it needs it. Since our inner selves know precisely what will impress the ego, they may choose to form a certain personality, insert him or her into physical reality, and help that person best personify the message our inner selves wish to get across to the masses. Jesus, Martin Luther King and Joan of Arc are good examples of this type of symbology, along with a myriad of other well-known and lesser-known personalities.

These methods of assistance by our inner selves are all well and good, and very appreciated. But what of the day-to-day, at times moment-by-moment help we need? How do we find the best path to a better paying job, a healthier body, a new piece of real estate? As usual our inner selves doesn't let us down.

Intuition or Bust

According to Seth, "The ego is not equipped to delve *directly* into nonphysical realities, but if it is trained to be flexible, it will accept such knowledge from other wider horizons of the self."[7] So, the ego is not meant to reach into the multi-dimensional aspects of the self, to use its faculties to probe the interior world. It takes a quieter portion of our being to approach the task of consciously exploring inner reality. However, the mature ego is one which will *accept* data from the interior world. In fact, that's part of its job, to receive and interpret impressions.

But most of the egos of today's world will only accept data from outside themselves. Indeed, they so mistrust their intuitions that they consciously choose to block information that doesn't fit into the framework of reality they accept as valid. Our egos have been taught since childhood that kosher information comes solely from the exterior world of facts and figures.

However, this is an extremely counterproductive stance to take; counterproductive, that is, if they want to experience a fulfilling life. Seth says, "Such a situation denies the individual his full strength, and cuts him off—consciously, now—from the important sources of his being. These conditions inhibit creative expression in particular, and deny the conscious self the continually emerging insights and intuitions otherwise unavailable."[8] Seth goes on to say that illusionary divisions then appear in the self, and the ego feels more alienated than ever.

The mission of all personalities, if they choose to accept it, is to loosen the ego's hold on what it will and will not allow as real. It's not an impossible mission, though. The ego can be taught to accept inner experiences while still retaining its analytical stance and outward regulatory function. The two are not in conflict. Seth calls the intellect brilliant, so it's not like he's suggesting it be set aside or replaced with the more esoteric forms of data gathering.

"The intellect alone cannot understand what the intuitions most certainly know,"[9] Seth tells us. The intellect and intuitions go hand in hand. Both are valuable to the whole picture of personal growth. According to our cosmic buddy, "Logic deals with exterior conditions, with cause-and-effect relationships. Intuitions deal with immediate experience of the most intimate nature, with subjective motions and activities that in your terms move far quicker than the speed of light, and with simultaneous events that your cause-and-effect level is far too slow to perceive."[10]

Intuition doesn't just magically appear in our lives once a year. Our inner selves guide us constantly, daily. They are very interested in helping us develop into the people we choose to be—they have a stake in our growth, you might say. So the onus is on them to flash insights into our minds that, if acknowledged by us, lead us in the direction of our desires. The bright ideas that light our minds, the voice with the answer to our dilemma, the breakthrough thought that leads us into new dimensions of the self, all of these come from our inner selves as intuition. We are handled with care by that deeper portion of our being, coddled and cuddled in ways we don't even realize. But intuition is not their only method of assistance.

Impulses Galore

One of the most underrated subjects of the times is impulses. Magazine articles on intuition are prolific, as are conferences and books. Intuition seems to grab people's attention. It has a kind of glamour, a diamond-bright aura about it that draws the intellect...and that the intellect can accept. But impulses? Ugh! They make us think of the chocolate cake we couldn't leave alone, the purchased shoes we could hardly afford, the chillingly unfamiliar bed in which we awoke.

Impulses don't deserve the bum rap they've been handed. Instead, they should be placed on the pedestal of knowledge and studied with great care, because impulses are the springboards to significant personal and world value fulfillment. Seth and Jane Roberts wrote the most extraordinary stuff about the nature of impulses in a "keeper" book called *The Individual and the Nature of Mass Events*. Because of Seth's perspective outside time and space and his deeper knowledge of how physical reality functions, he brings insights to impulses we'd simply never understand without his frame of reference. For instance, he says, "Ideally, by following your impulses you would feel the shape, the impulsive shape...of your life. You would not spend time wondering what your purpose was, for it would make itself known to you, as you perceived the direction in which your natural impulses led, and felt yourself exert power in the world through such actions. Again, impulses are doorways to action, satisfaction, the exertion of natural mental and physical power, the avenue for your private expression..."[11]

Let's go back to our inner self for a moment. By now it's clear it holds a much greater understanding of where we are and what we wish to accomplish during this lifetime than the conscious part of us in physical reality might know in any one isolated moment of time. In other words, our inner self sees all probabilities that surround us, what we've chosen to call the past and present, and the choices we can make that will eventually be called the future. It knows our belief system inside out; it knows our desires, our goals, our focus. It also knows our overall purpose and intent for this lifetime, the desires set before birth that we wish to accomplish this time around. There is no one else in the universe, including our conscious self, who so intimately knows us.

Now here we are, in physical reality with an eye trained on the exterior. We go about our days, taking care of business as events arise to meet us, living our lives from the moment point. We're not exactly prepared to make conscious daily decisions that take into consideration the complexity of developing a life we'd like to review after death and of which we'd be able to say, yeah, I did what I set out to do and had a fine time accomplishing it all.

But our inner self is. It's true it creates the events we wish to meet in life, but don't forget we have free will. So, our inner self may have a spectacular possibility ready to enter today's event stream, but through free will—and lack of understanding impulses—we may walk in another direction altogether. Literally. Say we're an architectural student in the local university, and for months we've been desiring to see the interior of a famous old mansion not usually open to the public. One fine day we're hurrying along our usual route to class when we have an impulse to veer right instead of to our normal left. *No*, we think, *I'll continue on my way because I'd like to get a cup of coffee, and that will take a few extra minutes*. So on we go.

Now, in this scenario, what would have happened if we'd followed the impulse to veer right? It turns out our inner self had set the stage for us to run into our old friend Joe who, it just so happened, had been given an invitation for two to visit the interior of the mansion that afternoon for a special showing. Free will led us away from Joe. Free will led us to ignore an impulse that didn't seem to fit with what we consciously had planned that day. But our inner self knew of our desire to see the house, and it knew how we would use what we observed in the mansion to define our personal style of architecture as time flowed on.

Not that we blew it completely by not following that singular impulse. More than likely our inner self would supply another event at another time that would answer our desire. But will we follow the impulse it sends to us then, or not? That, dear Brutus, is always the question.

Impulses are different from intuition. They both come from the inner self, and both bring their own kind of information, but the purpose behind an impulse is to spark us into direct action. Impulses are natural nudges from our inner self, suggestions toward an action that will lead us to some level of fulfillment. They come from unconscious knowledge. Perhaps the impulse is to walk into a new grocery store, and the first item that meets our eye is the cake mix we've scouted the town trying to find. Or perhaps the impulse is to enter a certain sporting event against all advice, and there we meet the person who becomes our mentor throughout life. Both events bring their own kind of fulfillment, both enhance our life in some way. Both come from our inner self in response to our own best interests, because it knows what we want and how to lead us to it.

But equally important, by following our impulses into action, we impress the world with our stamp of individuality. Seth says, "Through your mundane conscious choices, you affect all of the events of your world, so that the mass world is the result of multitudinous individual choices. You could not make choices at all if you did not feel impulses to do this or that, so that choices usually involve you in making decisions between various impulses."[12]

And that leads to a very significant point. If we have the desire to be wealthy, our inner self immediately starts putting the pieces into place outside time and space. Then it feeds impulses into our life for us to follow that lead to our pot of gold. At the same time, however, our desire to be financially set may be in conflict with how we see our self, how we feel about money, our definition of greed, etc. These beliefs may also set a desire in place to forego wealth. Now what does our inner self do? It sends us impulses that fit both scenarios, and it's up to us to choose the ones we wish to experience.

So, the question is, how do we choose the ones that lead to abundance? This is not a quick question to answer, because it involves understanding and changing beliefs, and a whole lot more. My book *Ten Thousand Whispers: A Guide to Conscious Creation* addresses the issue head on; in fact, that's its purpose. For now, just be aware that *any* direction you set for yourself through your beliefs, focus, intent and desire will automatically carry within it the impulses that will lead you to the goal. Ergo the chocolate cake, the new shoes that strain the budget, the compromised bed.

The "out" for us is that our inner self leans in our direction. It truly wants the best for us, however that's defined. If eating a whole cake in one sitting is not to our benefit, it will suggest, through impulse, how to avoid it next time. Where will our free will take us? And will we get lost in a jumble of contradictory impulses along the way?

The last thing we want to do is tremble at the thought of impulses. They've been given a bad name by a lot of people, who usually reference criminals, teenagers and cults as the ultimate in expression of impulses. However, Seth says what has happened when a person or group lashes out in a non-beneficial way is the result of the "power of impulses denied." He says these people have repressed well-intentioned impulses for so long that the repression finally leads to a blast of activity—usually in the wrong direction.

Impulses are urges toward action; and action cannot be denied. It can be ignored until it cannot be confined within good manners, but action will occur one way or another in this reality, which is, after all, based on action. While many people who are out of step with the mores of peaceful civilization will say they are acting out their power, Seth contends it's just the opposite; they are acting out of powerlessness. However, if they'd followed the impulses they had blindly ignored for so long, there would have been no need to feel powerless, because they would not have met the circumstances that reflected the condition in the first place.

And, by the way, Seth's not just talking about the more obvious radical departures from healthy actions that meet us face to face as newspaper headlines; he's talking about the feelings of powerlessness and hopelessness that perhaps each of us feels at some time in our life, whether it be on the job, on the streets, in our homes, in our schools or anywhere else. We're not off the hook of non-productive impulses, it seems, with simply the more obvious "offenders" left dangling. Any time we exhibit behavior contrary to our own or others' well being, we should question the internal path that led us there.

And in ending we go back to the source: "There are many schools for spiritual advancement that teach you to 'get rid of the clutter of your impulses and desires,' to shove aside the self that you are in search of a greater idealized version...but (the) inner self, which is the source of your present being, speaks through your impulses. They provide inbuilt spiritual and biological impetuses toward your most ideal development. You must trust the self that you are. Now."[13]

Dream Centers

Fortunately, there's another way the inner self bails us out of problems...fortunately, because this way bypasses the conscious self and works directly with the part of us that comes awake in the dream state. The ego doesn't have to interpret a thing to get this kind of assistance at the time it's happening; but later, in waking life, the ego does have to allow its intuitions and impulses full reign so the material can filter into physical reality. But I'm getting ahead of myself.

The daytime conscious self becomes the nighttime unconscious self, and vice versa, in a move designed by our inner self to work more closely with the combined aspects of the personality. The dream state is not a chaotic, illogical romp through the subconscious, as some think. It is highly specific in its purpose and constructed with utmost care... and much assistance takes place within it. Seth says, "In the...deep protected areas of sleep, the higher centers of the inner self are allowed to function and come to the aid of the three-dimensionally oriented portion of the personality. This more liberated self sees the situation much more clearly, suggests a given line of action (but does not order it), and informs the dreaming self. The dreaming self then manufactures a group of dreams in which the solution is stated within a symbolic dream situation."[14]

In essence, the inner self takes over in the dream state as director of our perceptions, temporarily replacing the ego. Since it is intimately familiar with us and our challenges, it knows what to do about them that will suit our personality. Armed with this knowledge, on a nightly basis our inner self sets about designing events we may, if we choose, try on for size. Some of what we learn in the dream roles we manufacture for ourselves will reach us as intuition, insight and impulses over the course of days following the dreams. And some will enter our lives as events that *match* the dream.

That's because what we try on in the dream state can be chosen to become part of our waking reality. In other words, we decide which scenario we wish to experience in physical life, and then our inner self goes about making it happen.

The point here is that not only is the wake-a-day person given assistance in different ways by his or her inner self, but so is the dream-a-night person. The helping hand never goes away. We just have to believe it, and have *faith* it will be there for us when we need it.

And with that segue, maestro...

Divine Glue

The natural order of the universe is held together by a secret ingredient. Consciousness, in any form and in any reality, can muck up its creations, sometimes to the point where the self loses its sense of security and excitement with life. William James feels that's what happened to him while in physical reality. Upon death, he came to understand what the secret ingredient is that makes our lives flow easily and with fulfillment—and what was lacking in his. It turns out to be faith.

Faith! Oh, no. Are we required to sign on the universal dotted line that we'll pledge allegiance to this or that brand of doctrine before we can reach heavenly peace? No, never again. The faith James is talking about has nothing to do with a belief in objects, disciplines or organizations. It has everything to do with the medium that supports and encourages growth of any kind.

Because we live in a reality constructed of thought, and because we don't understand or know the implications of what that means to us, we create very unfortunate events at times. With each uneasy situation we chip away at our natural buoyancy toward life until little remains except resignation and varying levels of anxiety.

In order for consciousness—any consciousness, any-where—to allow itself to move forward through experiences, it must feel safe. Since consciousness gets to choose how it thinks and feels, and what it experiences based on those thoughts and feelings, it sometimes gets wrapped up in its own underwear, so to speak. It gets lost in its anxiety and concern, and muddles around in dark nights of the soul.

But All That Is is nothing if not wise. It knew all the possibilities facing individualized consciousness, and it knew it had better provide a safety net for those times when uneasiness would set in. So All That Is permeated existence with faith. William James sensed it immediately upon death. He wonders, in fact, how he'd missed faith's obvious presence while he was physical. He concludes that he had believed faith to be a commitment of spirit to something outside one's self—a theology, philosophy, object or person—when it really has nothing to do with such things.

James sums up his new definition of faith this way: "To the extent that faith applies *to* anything, then it is trust in one's natural order of being; the feeling that the conditions for existence are largely conducive to it; that needs will be met within the circumstances of that natural order; and that one is couched and supported in one's existence by some larger Nature from which the natural order springs. In such a medium, bones, frogs, stars—and philosophers—grow."[15]

Nothing happens without the impetus of faith behind it. Faith provides the medium for growth and movement. It is a very real guiding light that consciousness uses as a beacon that leads to safety and fulfillment. It doesn't have to be sought like lost treasure; as we said, it permeates existence already. James says, "In my present environment...faith everywhere surrounds me, so that its support is one of the most outstanding elements of my existence. There is a complete lack of threatening conditions of any kind. I would have imagined such a state to be lacking also in challenge and creativity. Instead, I am filled with a sense of wonder, curiosity, and impetus that is never tiring. So natural do I now find this faith that it is hard to believe it was not a conscious part of my mental constitution during life."[16]

Faith, the divine glue that holds the universe together, is there for consciousness. It's part of the loving condition that is All That Is, it's the stuff that sustains life. There is no way to discuss consciousness and its various states and possibilities without recognizing the crucial role faith plays in the success of its explorations.

Toward a New Psychology

In the last chapter we suggested that a new science could develop from Seth's concepts defining the structure of the universe, and how our reality is created from the building blocks of consciousness. Is it not obvious from everything that's been said so far that a new psychology could also evolve, one based on a completely different understanding of the dimensions of the self? Jane Roberts says, "The Seth Material maintains that Freud's discovery of the subconscious represents only the first exploratory recognition of the whole inner self. Freud and Jung, according to Seth, only touched on the most obvious portions of what could be called 'Undiscovered Man' or the 'whole self.'"[17] And Seth says, "Jung's collective unconscious was an attempt to give your world its psychological roots, but Jung could not perceive the clarity, organization, and deeper context in which that collective unconscious has its own existence."[18] So much more territory needs to be explored by psychologists—the expanded inner territory that will carry them far beyond the compilation of today's thought.

A new psychology would be based on the acceptance of the inner self, and everything that flows from that acceptance. It would take into account our origins outside time and space, why we chose to become physical in this exact moment of history, the true roles of the conscious and subconscious minds, and the ego. It would understand the interrelationship between counterparts, probable selves and reincarnational selves, would know of their simultaneous existences, and would explore the passing of information between them. It would question why a soul would choose the circumstances of its birth and what beliefs might have led to or developed from the selection of its birth environment. It would know how the mind creates its reality based on what it expects to see, and therefore understand that what one experiences is not the cause, but the effect—and would handle the situation accordingly, without assigning victim or aggressor status to the drama's players, and instead focus on correcting the ego's misinterpretation of the exterior reality.

What a wonderful opportunity awaits the field of psychology. It is now in a position to make massive strides toward truly helping people to change, once and for all...and for the good of all.

A Parting Word...

According to our metaphysical expert, "All That Is speaks to all of Its parts, not with sounds, trumpets, and fanfare from without, but communicates Its messages through the living soul-stuff of each consciousness."[19] All That Is talks to us softly through our inner self, and it has since it formed individualized consciousness. So, it's not like the inner self is a new manifestation striding into twentieth-century life with the sole purpose of leading our world out of chaos. Indeed, Seth says the myths of guardian angels and fairy godmothers developed from humankind's intuitive understanding of this deeper, protective portion of itself. But the time has come—quite clearly come—when we must consciously acknowledge and communicate with the energy that sustains us and our reality.

The extent that we can loosen the ego's fear of being alone suggests the extent to which we will allow our intuition and knowledge of our multidimensional heritage to surface, and the extent to which we will live our lives more fully and contentedly, with new insights, added energy and more creativity at our fingertips. We can either move forward into a whole new era of life on earth, or we can continue the way we have for centuries. Acceptance of the inner self is the bridge between the worn and the glorious.

A parting word from Seth for the closing of this chapter encapsulates the most important idea that flows through it, because it stresses the key that unlocks the future. The highlighting is mine.

> "I cannot say this too often—you are far more than the conscious mind, and the self which you do not admit is the portion that not only insures your own physical survival in the physical universe which it has made, but which is also the connective between yourself and inner reality . . .

> "It is only through the recognition of the inner self that the race of man will ever use its potential."[20]

4

Value fulfillment is a psychological and physical propensity that exists in each unit of consciousness, propelling it toward its own greatest fulfillment in such a way that its individual fulfillment also adds to the best possible development on the part of each other such unit of consciousness.

—*Seth*, The Individual and the Nature of Mass Events, *Session 868*

Stretching Toward Value Fulfillment

In *The Afterdeath Journal of an American Philosopher*, William James discusses how consciousnesses that reside outside time and space come together for specific reasons. He says, "There are, again, other groupings of consciousness, alliances in which identities group together psychologically, as people do on earth, physically, in nations. These consciousnesses retain individuality while joining together in joint purposes, pooling separate viewpoints into psychic composites that I do not pretend to understand."[1]

This "joining together in joint purpose" isn't just limited to nonphysical consciousnesses; indeed it's what happens to consciousness in physical reality, also. Each civilization has a purpose in being, as does each individual. In general, Seth says as a group we're here to "aid in the great expansion of consciousness." Just like William James's after-death compatriots, we also are here together to pool our separate viewpoints into psychic composites. We form ourselves into nations and cities, into social, political, business and other groupings, and into families and couples. We have different viewpoints to offer each group, and things to learn that can be learned no other way.

Just as individual thoughts and beliefs create individual realities, so do group thoughts and beliefs create world reality. The inner realities of our composite psyches give birth to all mass events. Seth emphasizes the idea in this quote: "...The magnification of individual reality combines and enlarges to form vast mass reactions—such as, say, the initiation of an obviously new historical and cultural period; the rise of governments; the birth of a new religion...; mass conversions; mass murders in the form of wars; the sudden sweep of deadly epidemics; the scourge of earthquakes, floods, or other disasters; the inexplicable appearance of periods of great art or architecture or technology."[2]

As consciousness in physical form, we do it all, and we do it together. Consciousness doesn't create in a vacuum. Earth life was set up as a cooperative reality, meaning there is constant interaction between all life forms. Sure, individually we're learning to translate our thoughts into objectified results, but we're also learning to take responsibility for the impact of those results, and that necessitates an interweaving with others. We play out our ideas for all to see, at times sharing events intimately, and at other times staying less entwined.

Basically why we're in physical reality is to develop a deeper understanding of our immense creativity through individual and joint expression. Seth says, "Your power as a rational consciousness focused in the present provides you with opportunities for creativity that you are but vaguely learning to understand. As you <u>do</u> learn, you will automatically begin to appreciate the multidimensional nature of not only your own species but of others as well."[3]

However, there is another reason we, as consciousness, chose physical reality, and it has to do with what Seth calls value fulfillment. In *Dreams, "Evolution," and Value Fulfillment*, Jane Roberts makes this comment in Essay 1: "Seth uses the term 'value fulfillment'...to imply life's greater values and characteristics—that is, we are alive not only to continue to insure life's existence, but to add to the very quality of life itself. We do not just receive the torch of life and pass it on as one Olympic runner does to another, but we each add to that living torch or flame a power, a meaning, a quality that is uniquely our own." Seth goes on to clarify the concept: "(Value fulfillment) means simply that each form of life seeks toward the fulfillment and unfolding of all of the capacities that it senses within its living framework, knowing that in that individual fulfillment each other species of life is also benefited."[4]

The expression of value fulfillment is what nudges us on toward accomplishment and pleasure, toward a broader horizon of ideas and a desire to deepen our spiritual understandings. It's the thread that weaves us together, humans and all other species, because it's the shared stuff of our souls. The world is working properly when every living form experiences value fulfillment.

So, when we enter life on earth we seek to express our creativity in as many directions as brings us value fulfillment. But what does that mean from a practical standpoint? Consciousness is infinitely creative, so we can't possibly experience in one lifetime the full dimensions of our being. Do we define certain areas of development, then, before we're born, areas individual to us that we wish to explore this time around in our constant movement toward and through value fulfillment? Sure. When we enter the fray of physical life, we do so with objectives and goals in mind. Certainly our desire is to grow our understanding about the creative abilities of consciousness...ours in particular. But like a delicious chocolate parfait, there are other layers of purpose to be tasted and enjoyed. We come to physicality with a generalized plan of action established and hopes defined, and then we let the drama roll.

Actually, it all starts rolling prior to conception.

Starting Out Small

The miracle of human birth touches us, male and female alike, on deep levels. We stand in awe of the process that brings a new soul into existence. Science seems to have a good handle on the mechanics of the process, being able to track the growth of a fetus virtually from conception to birth. But the conception point from which doctors start the tracking process is not the primary time of genesis for a new human being. It starts when the decision is made by a greater self to enter a portion of its consciousness into physical reality. After the decision is made, the mental and physical characteristics of the new soul are agreed upon by the personality-to-be and its inner self, its initial belief structure is determined and its environment and parents selected. Then an enormous charge of energy is experienced that allows for the initial breakthrough into matter as a fetus. The greater self has once again sent a portion of itself into physical reality to learn and grow—and seek value fulfillment.

Seth says that at no other time in a person's life is so much energy intently, purposefully directed as when the fetus is being formed and developed in the womb. The personality-to-be faces the great task of converting infinite data into a physical structure, and while most of the work is accomplished by the third month of pregnancy, it continues at a heightened intensity through birth, and beyond. Natural abortions occur when difficulties in construction are experienced by the developing personality, and its greater self suggests it not continue the process until a later time.

(Jane Roberts had a miscarriage early in her marriage to Rob Butts, and Seth later told them the fetus had changed its mind, and had chosen to withdraw from physicality. He commented at another time that the consciousness of a fetus cannot be destroyed by abortion, natural or calculated.)

While still a fetus, a personality is in telepathic communication not only with its parents, but with animals and other people. Seth says, "The fetus...will also react to the death of an animal in the family, and will be acquainted with the unconscious psychic relationships within the family long before it reaches the sixth month."[5]

Interestingly, Seth notes that a fetus literally sees through its eyelids and its mother's body, that it sees shape and form and responds to light. And, just as interestingly, it sees more than adults do. This is because the fetus does not know what restrictions are placed on what it can and cannot observe as forms in its reality, so it sees them all. As it grows closer to birth, and then afterwards, a baby comes to understand that what its parents see is what it needs to see—and no more—and so it starts to drop the images that don't conform to its parents' reality. It begins to build its environment to match that of its parents; in other words, it casts out equally valid, but not accepted, structures.

During the time the fetus sees extraneous forms not materialized by its parents, it also picks up sound from that extended reality. Voices and other sounds reach it in the womb from both the physical reality of its parents and their not-chosen realities. These overlays of sight and sound actually follow the baby into the world, but because confusion results (which is usually interpreted by its parents as disorientation) the baby quickly teaches itself to perceive only the official picture presented to it. In other words, the new little human being learns to focus itself specifically into physical reality from greater dimensions.

Setting the Stage of Life

The newborn baby enters physical reality through intense and infinite machinations. Significant attention has been placed on the formation of the infant, both from a body and a spirit standpoint. So, what about its mind, its personality, its psyche? Are they formed willy-nilly, or is precise detail afforded them also? After all we've learned about consciousness so far, this is a no-brainer.

The conscious mind exists before birth and after death. It is part of the soul, or greater self, and it is jam-packed with information before an infant's head enters the birth canal. Seth says, "When you arrive, or emerge, into physical life, not only is your mind *not* a blank slate, waiting for the scrolls that experience will write upon it, but you are already equipped with a memory bank far surpassing that of any computer. You face your first day upon the planet with skills and abilities already built in, though they may or may not be used; and they are not merely the result of heredity..."[6]

Prior to our decision to reincarnate, we choose the abilities we wish to explore and the challenges we will face, in general terms. They vary significantly between individuals. No human sets up the same slate of personality and direction as another, because we're on our own journeys through time and space toward value fulfillment, unmatched by any other soul, ever. That's how unique we are, and how important. Each of us has specific reasons for choosing the course we set for ourselves, because in some way it adds to or magnifies the whole. There is not a soul that has lived on the face of the earth who was not born with immense purpose and meaning behind its birth.

Because of that focused purpose, we carefully choose our parents and families, our immediate birth environment and the circumstances of our physical body (from our sex, biological race, and bodily characteristics, to any physical disabilities). Usually, by definition, those choices suggest or outline the challenges we have set to overcome and results we wish to reach. In other words, we set up a framework through which we can meet experiences that will allow us to develop our abilities and fulfill our desires. Our progress is measured by the ways and means we use in solving, or not solving, our problems.

However—and this is a big however—we are not at the mercy of pre-set circumstances. We have been given free will specifically so we can change our minds about what we wish to experience. If we don't like where we are in life, then through our great creativity, we can change it. As Seth says, "The creative power to form your own experience is within you now, as it has been since the time of your birth and before. You may have chosen a particular theme for this existence, a certain framework of conditions, but within these you have the freedom to experiment, create, and alter conditions and events. Each person chooses for himself the individual patterns <u>within which</u> he will create this personal reality. But inside these bounds are infinite varieties of actions and unlimited resources."[7]

This is a very important point that's missed by many people when they seek to consciously recognize their soul's purpose or direction. They assume they were placed on earth to become, say, a singer or a fisherman or a spiritual leader. First of all, they were not "placed on earth": they placed themselves on earth—a fine line between meanings, but nonetheless important. One suggests a power outside themselves deigned they would become something or somebody. The other suggests it's not a destiny thing with godlike blessings behind it...except, of course, their own godly choices.

The second issue is that while a person may have wanted to explore singing in this life, her blueprint includes other talents and desires she could choose to actualize in her primary reality instead. In other words, we don't run amok in life if we overstep a one-and-only path decreed by our greater self. There are many paths that lead individuals to value fulfillment, and they vary greatly. And don't forget, each person has multiple probable selves, and each self will seek its own pattern of development. So, if we choose not to become the singer, the singer goes off and does her thing in another reality.

A very good example of this came from the life of Jane Roberts. Jane was raised in the Catholic Church and became a devout young girl. At the same time, she had a strong mystical nature. According to Seth, when Jane was 12 years old, an intersection of probabilities occurred. One young Jane became a nun, still able to express her mysticism but snugly confined within acceptable religious standards. Another Jane became the mystic that is part of the reality we all share, the Jane who overcame the dogma of the church and allowed her mystical nature to expand and develop.

Seth explains it this way: "In your terms, the intersection with probabilities occurred one day in an interview the child had with a priest...The child in seventh or eighth grade wrote a poem, expressing the desire to be a nun, and brought it to a parish priest. In your probability, the priest told the child that she was needed by her mother; but intuitively he saw that (Jane's) mysticism would not fit into the church organization. In the other probability, (Jane's) desire at that time won. (She) managed to water down the extent and dimensions of (her) mysticism enough so that it was acceptable (to the church)."[8]

But, can we get so far off track that we overshoot most of our blueprint and do not accomplish much in the way of our pre-birth desires? Unfortunately, yes. Free will is an interesting phenomenon. It's what allows us to use our creativity fully, choosing this, then that, to manifest and experience. What we choose will be based on our beliefs and intent, and if our beliefs are extremely limiting and our intent negative, we automatically clamp down on personal growth. We, in essence, have chosen by default to ignore the greater possibilities or scope of our blueprint.

As a world race and species, we can do the same thing. Individuals aren't the only ones with blueprints or goals they are attempting to achieve. Collectively we have set our sights on certain developments that further our civilization along a generalized desired path, and collectively we can bypass the blueprint and create a new one. Whether or not we like the blueprint we're creating becomes the issue. Indeed, it's the question in the minds of many in the world today.

Cooperative Interaction

Before we are born into physicality, we are updated on the historical time frame we've chosen to explore and the world conditions of the day. We're made aware of the general themes of the times and the active beliefs that are presently developing those themes. Some of us choose to align ourselves with those mass beliefs, others choose to play the Devil's advocate in some areas, yet go along with the crowd in others. We define our positions based on our purposes and intent for this present life…and our purposes and intent will be reflected onto our global life as well as our personal one.

For instance, a soul who holds the belief in victimization

may choose to be born into a culture where his native nationality is abhorrent to the majority of his countrymen. Effectively, he has placed himself in the position of becoming a probable victim at some point in his life. His personal belief in victimization will also serve a world view, however. Many such people may join him in his chosen time and place, all feeling they are in some way vulnerable to the ruling forces.

A conflict may arise where the powers-that-be (who, of course, hold their own sets of beliefs) try to destroy our friend and his cohorts. The drama is played out on the global stage for all to see, with the express purpose of bringing the limiting beliefs of both sides to the attention of the world consciousness. To what avail? So those who did not directly participate in the conflagration can experience their own thoughts, feelings and beliefs around the event. To what avail? So they can modify their personal positions to ones that are more moderate, or more understanding, or more loving, if necessary. To what avail? So their new beliefs will feed into the whole world consciousness and help modify the beliefs of the masses. To what avail? So that value fulfillment flows through all life unimpeded.

And what of our friend, the victim? Can he change his mind about his assumed role? At any time. All he has to do is start seeing himself differently (i.e., change his beliefs to ones more reflective of personal power and self-worth), and his situation will alter. He may find himself transferred out of the conflict area, or come into an inheritance that allows him to buy a ticket to somewhere else. Or he may stay where he is and yet find he's not physically impacted by the ruling class. Indeed, our friend could find that he becomes an agent for change in his country, because he no longer harbors fears that keep him in a subservient position. Now he is free to act and react from a position of power...*self power.*

But through it all, our victim was in constant psychic contact with every other player in the event which was evolving. According to Seth, "An event involving (say) a job change concerns motion on the part of many people, and implies a network of communications on the part of all of the inner (selves) involved. Obviously, then, a mass physical event implies an inner system of communication of proportions that would put your technological communications to shame."[9]

Value Fulfillment For All

To truly gain a sense of the magnificence of consciousness takes a more complete understanding of how our world is created. We look at the accomplishments of our civilization—our technologies, cities, cultural life, sciences, etc.—and marvel at the use of the intellect that brought them about. However, without infinite activities of consciousness underlying physical reality, none of our accomplishments could have happened in the first place.

To quote Seth: "There are organizations of consciousness...that leapfrog the species, that produce no arts or sciences per se—yet these together form the living body of the earth and the physical creatures thereon. Their products are the seas upon which you sail your ships, the skies through which your airplanes fly, the land upon which your cities sprawl, and the very reality that makes your culture, or any culture, possible."[10]

Our inner selves are part of that "trans-species consciousness," as Seth calls it, and so are we. He says not only is man part of this psychological gestalt, but so are plants and animals, even though none of us have chosen to perceive our participation in it. What this means is that our natural world is formed by all species of earth-tuned consciousness, along with other consciousnesses not primarily focused in physical reality. And what it also means it that each of us, and the animals and the rest of nature, work in concert to create a global environment in which we can all live cooperatively.

Cooperation is a key word. On one level of consciousness, we joyfully participate as a whole to create our world, right down to the varied personalities of certain geographical areas. (Seth says, "Any section of the land has an identity, so to speak, and I am not talking symbolically. Such identities represent the combined organizations of consciousness of land, man, and animal, within any given realm."[11]) Unconscious cooperation pulls off an infinity of constant creation between species. Oh, if we could only see the symmetry of it all and work in *conscious, knowing* concert with the animals and nature.

How insufferably superior humankind has become since Darwin described his theory of evolution. Top of the heap, that's us, the big shots of the world. It's our right, based on our "obvious" rung on the evolutionary ladder, to be cruel, uncaring and destructive to animals and nature. If they get in our way, hey, what's a bloke to do but walk all over them?

Seth knocks us down a peg or two—or twenty or thirty—when he describes the panorama of interaction among all species, interaction so necessary to the experience of value fulfillment on planet earth. He says, "The reasoning mind, as you have used it, considers that only reasoning creatures are capable of understanding life's values. Other forms of life have almost seemed beside the point, their value considered only insofar as they were of service to man. But man's life is obviously dependent upon the existence of life's other species, and with him those species share certain values. Life is sacred—all life—and, again, all life seeks value fulfillment, not simply physical survival."[12]

If All That Is forms and is within everything, and if our

inner selves create our *complete* reality from the soul stuff of consciousness, animals and plants are as vital to the universe as humans are. They are composed of consciousness units, alive and aware and striving for conditions that best suit their desires. They are eternal, along with us. Seth says, "You are not separated from the animals and the rest of existence by virtue of possessing an eternal inner consciousness. Such a consciousness is present within all living beings, and in all forms."[13]

Anyone who has shared a household or farm with animals knows quite well that animals have feelings. They show affection, loyalty, pleasure and contentment, among other things. So how has science been able to use animals for testing purposes, bringing pain and anguish to them with barely a stirring of conscience? William James sheds light on this question with the following: "...Science has so objectified the animals that it has closed its eyes to the animals' reality of feeling and, yes, sentiment. Stressing the theories of conventional evolution and its objective considerations, science has completely overlooked the greatest factor in creature life: the very sensations of creaturehood and the vast communications that exist among all species. I do not mean to overromanticize, yet overromanticization is a far lesser error than an overobjectification that dismisses life's sentimental quality as beside the point, and justifies cruelty to animals by citing distorted evolutionary concepts."[14]

And Seth has this to say about science and its use of animals in testing: "In many cases your scientists seem to have the strange idea that you can understand a reality by destroying it; that you can perceive the life mechanism of an animal by killing it; or that you can examine a phenomenon best by separating yourself from it. So, often, you attempt to examine the nature of the brain in man by destroying the brains of animals, by separating portions of the animal brain from its components, isolating them, and tampering with the overall integrity of both the animal in question and of your own spiritual processes. By this I mean that each such attempt puts you more out of context, so to speak, with yourself and your environment, and other species. While you may 'learn' certain so-called facts, you are driven still further away from any great knowledge, because the so-called facts stand in your way. You do <u>not</u> as yet understand the uniqueness of consciousness."[15]

Of course, science isn't the only perpetrator of cruelty to animals. Unfortunately, it happens daily, in homey settings. A dog gets whipped for falling out of grace, a deer gets killed because it eats the prize flowers, a kitten dies in an airless sun-soaked car. We usually don't have to look too far from our own backyards to find hurting animals.

Love, intent, desire and purpose are what drive all consciousness toward value fulfillment, according to Seth. If any of the four are missing, or blocked for some reason, consciousness usually chooses not to continue in physical reality. In other words, if a certain quality of life is lacking, plants, animals and humans feel it strongly, and make their decisions accordingly. Kittens and puppies, for instance, will choose to die, many times through a disease, to make a statement that either their private lives or those of their "brothers and sisters" *en masse* are significantly lacking in the ability to be fulfilled; i.e., they feel unloved, unwanted, powerless. Trees or plants will choose to experience a killing parasite at times, in order to make a statement about how they or their species elsewhere in the world are being treated.

It always gets back to value fulfillment being the main motivation of consciousness, and not simply individual value fulfillment, but that of all species as well. And it always gets back to the bare fact that every living thing of earth carries the responsibility to be kind and thoughtful to every other living thing of earth. It's not a responsibility that demands all humans run out immediately and become activists for specific causes. But it is definitely a responsibility that demands we become more caring, more personal, more touched by nature and animals. Our loving thoughts and delighted sensations when animals enter our purview are very helpful, and very powerful. And a friendly, compassionate pat on the head doesn't hurt.

There is an even grander reaction, however, when we show love, camaraderie, and compassion to fellow humans and other species in the individual, private moments of our days. It seems there is an inner system of communication in which the cells of all living things are connected, and because of that connection, any gesture or thought of ours toward any consciousness on earth is immediately transferred to the whole. *All cellular life constantly communicates.* All cellular life exchanges information in an open-ended exploration of possibilities from which our natural world emerges. We join to create physical reality, and what we create is based on how each piece of consciousness <u>feels</u> about itself.

We are here to learn just what that means from a responsibility standpoint.

The Ultimate Healer

The aspirations, dreams and fears of consciousness intertwine to form the events of our world. To be precise, the *thought* behind our aspirations, dreams and fears forms our experience. Yet the strength and effectiveness of thought is seldom considered as an antidote to world problems. Once we understand the nature of physical reality, however, it becomes obvious that thought causes our problems and thought can make them go away...perhaps not overnight, but eventually. What else will, if not thought?

We cannot discount the impact of each individual's mental and psychic state on the world as a whole. William James brings the idea into focus via his perspective after death with these words: "I can follow thought's masses as they form above the world, mixing with others, flowing in patterns sometimes light, sometimes dark or dimming, and I can perceive the intensity of emotion that drives them. As a rain cloud will surely bring a shower, from my standpoint it is obvious that certain thought patterns will bring about physical events suiting their nature, so it is with considerable interest that I watch those emotional and mental patterns that surround the world...I do perceive the dawn of new ideas, the glow of peace or faith or contentment as these surround the earth, 'rising' amidst the darker forms of doubt and fear..."[16]

So, what do we do, individually and as a society, to head off or resolve mass events which mirror a despondent, depressed populace, or slice of populace? Seth suggests the following: "To anticipate danger, or to imaginatively take on the troubles of others robs you of the very energy with which you could help them. I am not saying...to turn your eyes from the unfortunate conditions of the world. Practical help is needed in all areas of human life. Yet it is far better, and more practical ultimately, to concentrate upon the beneficial elements of civilization—far better to organize your thoughts in areas of accomplishment than to make mental lists of man's deficiencies and lacks. Such a practice leads to feelings of helplessness and hopelessness, in which effective action seems impossible."[17] And I refer you to another quote from our psychic source of wisdom: "Life possesses an exuberance. If this is cherished, nurtured, encouraged, then additional energy is generated that is not needed for the purposes of daily private life—a superabundance, that can be effectively directed in those areas of the world where help is most needed...Your thoughts generate practical experience. When these change, conditions will change."[18]

As long as we believe we are at the mercy of circumstances out of our control, we will never be powerful enough to change our private existences, let alone major world conditions. Part of the solution is to educate ourselves about consciousness and value fulfillment, and learn, once and for all, the nature of this reality in which we find ourselves. Another part, obviously, is to apply the information to our lives in a practical manner.

5

In your system of reality you are learning what mental energy is, and how to use it. You do this by constantly transforming your thoughts and emotions into physical form. You are supposed to get a clear picture of your inner development by perceiving the exterior environment. What seems to be a perception, an objective concrete event independent from you, is instead the materialization of your own inner emotions, energy and mental environment.

—*Seth*, The Seth Material, *Chapter 10*

Weaving the Web of Magic

When All That Is created individualized consciousness and bade it go create, it wasn't just talking figuratively. Consciousness is imbued with the ability and desire to create...well, everything. Everything we see or experience, whether it is through a microscope, a telescope, an eye, a dream, is consciousness which has taken form. For its own reasons, consciousness decided it would become this, symbolize that, play a role, sound exquisite. It would form worlds and universes, and exterior lives and inner realities. And it would remain within the structures it created, transforming itself into them.

This is not news to you, but I'll state it one more time, because it's crucial that we come to believe it: We are consciousness, we are part of All That Is. We are a part of the creative force which builds worlds and realities. We literally create everything we experience, and we're in physical form to learn how to do it knowingly. We are magicians, wizards *extraordinarie*, as Jane Roberts expresses so eloquently in her poem, "Magic Show":

What magicians we all are,
turning darkness into light,
transforming invisible atoms
into the dazzling theater
of the world,
pulling objects,
(people as well
as rabbits)
out of secret
microscopic closets,
turning winter into summer,
making a palmful of moments
disappear through time's trap door.

We learned the methods
so long ago
that they're unconscious,
and we've hypnotized ourselves
into believing
that we're the audience,
so I wonder where we served
our apprenticeship.
Under what master magicians did we learn
to form reality
so smoothly that we forgot to tell ourselves
the secret?

Creating a Magical Reality

Physical reality is a "place" which consciousness uses to teach itself about the power of focused energy. Consciousness thinks things into existence, no matter where it resides. Physical reality is a psychological medium constructed by consciousness, for consciousness, as a place to experiment with the energy of thought and see what happens...slowly.

When we're outside of time and space, our ideas are constructed into some kind of form instantaneously upon thinking them. A tricky and potentially chaotic situation indeed, if a consciousness doesn't possess the finesse and skill to handle such conditions. So, in all their wisdom, our collective inner selves called a cosmic meeting. The subject: what to do with consciousnesses which had not learned the tricks of their trade enough to ply them consciously and with precision in simultaneous time. The solution: design an environment where they would still use the power of thought to create experiences, but one which would give these consciousnesses the opportunity to see each of their creations one at a time, instead of simultaneously. The purpose: to allow them time to analyze the results of their constructions and determine whether or not they liked what they had created. The conclusion: a reality would be honed with linear time as a root assumption, or an assumed structure. This structure would support the concept of discrete space-time slots for each idea construction.

A description of physical reality as one "place" is very misleading, though. It sounds singular, as if there were but one reality that all souls inhabit while present on earth Yet that's not the case. According to Seth, we each reside in our own private space continuum, and that's where we play out our life. Our space continuum is our own reality, and technically we never enter another's. In *The Seth Material*, Seth uses the example of a glass sitting on a coffee table in a room occupied by three people.

He says there is not just one physical glass created by the consciousnesses of the three people, but that each person creates his or her own glass. Interestingly, he adds that the glasses are not identical, simply very similar, and each consciousness creates its glass through its own personal perspective. And this, of course, tells us why two people can view the same event yet see different details and outcomes. Through a selection process we decide just exactly what it is we wish to see, and then translate the appropriate energy into physical objects and events in our individual space continuums.

I choose the events I wish to experience, and in they come to my space continuum. You do the same. How, then, do we work together to create what seems to be a joint reality? One thing we do is hold the same assumptions within our private space continuums. We agree to agree that our exterior environments will match, in general terms. For instance, we agree on the geography and topography of the earth, the countries and cities spread around it, the history and language of each place, the locations of buildings within defined boundaries, the types of foods grown in different regions, the variety of weather conditions around the globe, etc. So, when I visit England in winter, I see the same things you do...again, generally speaking.

Groups of consciousnesses agree to form events, and then each individual decides on his or her personal level of participation. We play out each event of choice in our private space continuum, keeping shared details rather similar, designed from the same psychic pot of color and texture. As William James says, "...While each cast of consciousness forms its own picture, that picture is composed of the same physical propensities or physical field from which others also form their realities."[1]

Where we meet to discuss which events we'll jointly create is done outside time and space. One place is in the dream state, where most of the decisions are made. Another is when our primary consciousness is not focused in physical reality, but outside of it—which is about 50% of the time. According to Seth, we pulsate in and out of time and space on a moment-by-moment basis, meaning we're here as much as we're not. When we're not here, we're with our inner self, determining which events we'll next experience in our personal space continuum. Then we telepathically ask certain people to actively participate, if they choose to, in our event. Some will, some won't.

If it's critical we have a player for a given scene, some cooperative consciousness will eventually agree to the role. For instance, we're never without someone, somewhere, to love us or hate us, and anything in-between, depending on what we request via our attitudes, thoughts and feelings. Once our scene is set and the curtain is ready to rise, whoever has agreed to join the event taps into the pattern for it and dutifully copies that pattern into his or her space continuum.

From outside time and space, the stage is prepared for a three-dimensional event. In stunning cooperation, the consciousnesses involved have created the illusion of a joint reality and the environment to back it up.

Magic, no?

An Overview of Event Materialization

Any physical event enters our reality from "somewhere else." Events are symbolic interpretations of inner experiences that eventually coalesce in time and space. According to Seth, "Physical events imply the collection of basically nonphysical forces into an organization that exists initially outside of the time-space context. This is a psychological organization, consisting of a selection of chosen probable events. These wait in the wings, so to speak, for physical actualization."[2]

The dream state plays a significant role in the selection of the events we will eventually materialize. In what Seth calls the predream state, knowledge of possible events is given and personal drives and intents are studied. Eventually an event that meets our requirements is determined and analyzed for certain criteria: how it will fit into the mass framework of reality; its impact on others; and what future events could form out of it. Seth says, "In a dazzling display you are aware of such events from infinite perspectives. Consciously you could not grasp such information, much less act upon it…"[3]

Before entering our reality a selected event must fit within an appropriate space-time slot; have a certain amount of desire around it; be backed by our beliefs and thoughts; and be permeated with intensity. Then, Seth says, "The final trigger for that actualization may come from the waking or dream states, but it will represent the final factor needed— the quickening of inspiration, desire, or purpose—that will suddenly activate the initial psychological organization as a physical occurrence."[4]

Once the actualization trigger has been pulled, it becomes the brain's responsibility to translate the event into a physical structure through the application of the outer senses. The electromagnetic nature of an event is projected onto the brain by the inner self, and the brain reacts by activating one or more of the perceptive mechanisms—sight, touch, smell, taste, sound—which brings the event into actuality. According to Seth, "Momentarily a field of relatedness is set up that is highly charged, one that provides an inner path by which probable events can flow into your area of recognized events. This path exists on psychological levels, and triggers your perceptive mechanisms, which then of course react and dutifully perceive."[5]

It is also the brain's responsibility to organize selected events into some sort of linear orientation, taking them from their nonlinear source and placing them into a time line we can deal with—an illusory time line, but nonetheless a necessary reference system for three-dimensional reality.

Converting Thought to Reality

According to our metaphysical expert, "Ideas and feelings that you want made physical carry within them the mechanisms that will put them in the proper range, well within the electromagnetic field necessary for physical development."[6] The mechanisms Seth is talking about is what he calls electromagnetic energy (EE) units. He says that consciousness emanates these EE units with each subjective experience, or mental activity. That is, every time consciousness thinks a thought, expresses a feeling, senses its environment, or experiences any other kind of stimuli, EE units are automatically created and released. They rest, according to Seth, just beneath the range of physical matter.

EE units don't usually remain detached and alone for long. They are naturally drawn to others of their kind that have the same leanings or propensity, and as they find each other, they form groupings. If the groupings are imbued with enough intensity, they break through into physical reality. Seth says the psychological activity around a potential event builds up a charge that "allows purely mental acts to 'break the time-space barrier'" and emerge in a physical world.

But EE units are not the original impetus that propels events and matter outward; they are simply the main ingredient derived from the impetus. The impetus is thought and emotion. When enough EE units are built up (that is, when consciousness thinks a repetitive thought or holds a relatively constant feeling over a period of time), an event is formed as the EE units coalesce into a whole.

The EE units then trigger certain responses in the brain (which they create and permeate), and the brain reacts by perceiving the event suggested by the EE units. In other words, in comes a life event, one selected from the field of probabilities by a build-up of EE units, and one physically created by the senses controlled by the brain.

To clarify EE units, here's Seth: "Each thought or emotion therefore exists as an electromagnetic energy unit or as a combination of these under certain conditions, and often with the help of coordinate points, they emerge into the building blocks of physical matter...Mental images, accompanied by strong emotion, are blueprints therefore upon which a corresponding physical object, or condition or event, will in your terms appear."[7]

What exactly are the coordinate points mentioned by Seth that help propel EE units into physical reality? They are concentrated energy points that permeate physical reality. Seth says there are four absolute coordinate points that intersect *all* realities, and lesser powered ones called main coordinate points and subordinate points. All of them are accumulations of pure energy which act as transformers, and according to Seth, "provide much of the generating energy that makes creation continuous in your terms." They remain dormant until activated by highly charged EE units, and the energy of the originating thought or emotion is tremendously enhanced when it comes in contact with one of these power points. Through the energy of the various coordinate points, creation happens.

Seth goes into electromagnetic energy units and coordinate points in depth in his work, but the main concept for us to grasp from this brief description of them is that, as the psychic scientist tells us, "...Thoughts and emotions are formed into physical matter by very definite methods and through laws quite valid, though they may be presently unknown."[8] Thoughts and feelings definitely create. The sooner we truly understand that statement, the sooner we can build our lives and our world to our liking.

The Ongoing Life of Emotions

The subject of feelings, when viewed through the eyes of conventional thought, seems rather straightforward. When experienced, emotions may not be so easy to understand, but the idea that they are contained within the mind and body of the person who experiences them seems obvious enough to accept. However, as he does with many such societal assumptions, Seth blows the theory wide open.

Feelings and emotions are *not* contained within the mind, any more than thoughts are. Once expressed, they do something interesting: They come alive with purpose. They impress our outer and inner lives with their meaning and offer themselves up for study and exploration. The infinite variations and degrees of feelings we experience as consciousness in human form produce symbols in different stages of our awareness, from the physical to the soul level, at times becoming concrete items and at other times becoming psychological realities.

For instance, Seth says our immediate material environment alters, depending on what we're feeling. The emotion of the moment changes the objects surrounding us—literally. Feelings of joy and happiness help us to create our objects more vividly and as sharper images. Feelings of depression bring the walls closer together, dim the lights, and sift a dusty pall over our environment—again, quite literally. Our feelings are accurately translated into physical reality as part of our lives.

At the soul level, our feelings are picked up and translated not into symbols but as realities of emotion that are then explored. From this exercise the soul learns new methods of perception and expression that Seth says would have been utterly incomprehensible to it previously. In between the physical manifestation of feelings and the soul's pure perception of them are numerous other stages of exploration, each leading to a new freedom of expression.

For instance, in our daydreams and altered states of consciousness our feelings are given a wider range of play, without our usual restraints. This leads to their being woven into our dreams where we reach yet another level of understanding the power of feelings. After the dream state, our feelings enter a level of consciousness where it is unnecessary to use symbols at all to represent emotions, and creativity happens without the need for them.

Symbols are highly charged psychic structures. They represent inner realizations that have not been captured through direct comprehension. Therefore, they are great indicators as to the state of our consciousness at any given time, and they change shape with our subjective change. Today's symbol for our mother may be quite different than the one we use tomorrow.

There are no universal symbols we can count on to reflect humankind's inner structure of any given feeling, it seems, no collective symbology we can point to and say, if you dream of a bear it means such and such, or, if you develop a cold, it means thus and so. We individually choose our symbols on a deep level of consciousness, and they are crafted in the moment to match the moment's inner translation.

Just as changing our thoughts changes our life, so does changing our feelings alter our experience. Our immediate symbols metamorphose into something else, becoming a bright, shiny new moment full of potential, or a desired car we "finally" find. Learning to sense the inner coutours of our symbols, in dreams and while awake, can be of enormous assistance in deciphering the psychological meaning behind our manifested idea constructions.

The Power Place of the Universe

All of the activity that happens outside physical reality—the dream states, the decision states, the creation states, all of the inner intricacies that must take place prior to an experienced event—happens first in a psychological medium created by and a part of the vast network of consciousness which creates our reality. Seth calls this psychological medium Framework 2. First-line creation happens in Framework 2; its results then enter physical reality, or what the information man calls Framework 1.

Framework 2 is the workplace of our inner selves. It's here they arrange all the details, the chance encounters, the unexplained coincidences we meet in life before a desire of ours is finally actualized. Seth says, "It is as if Framework 2 contains an infinite information service that instantly puts you in contact with whatever knowledge you require, that sets up circuits between you and others, that computes probabilities with blinding speed. Not with the impersonality of a computer, however, but with a loving intent that has your best purposes in mind—yours and also those of each other individual."[9]

Framework 1, the outer dimension of reality, emerges from and yet is contained within Framework 2, the inner dimension of reality. Our material world overlaps Framework 2. Our inner selves tend to the creation of the events we specify from that medium. Since it is the source of our world, Framework 2 must hold all the knowledge our inner selves need to contend with the constant creation of physical reality. According to Seth, the information available to our inner selves in that psychological medium is infinite.

There are two very important characteristics of Framework 2 that impact us directly. One is that impediments don't exist there. Anything can be created in Framework 2 with ease by our inner selves, and inserted into Framework 1 with no problem. And the other is that Framework 2 is predisposed toward the creation of good events. In other words, it is not a neutral medium. It leans in favor of our fulfillment.

Take our friend from chapter 4, the victim of a coercive government. He fed his beliefs in vulnerability and victimization to his inner self through his conscious mind, and then in Framework 2 his inner self dutifully copied his feelings into representative symbols. Events entered his life which proved his victim status, he took them as accurate representations of reality, and that led him to continue the vulnerability cycle because the events seemed so much outside of his control.

Meanwhile other activity was taking place in Framework 2, also. Our friend's inner self was busily shaping more positive events to feed into Framework 1 that would remind him that he did indeed have the power to alter his life's conditions. Perhaps the events took the form of fresh thoughts of personal strength, or the determination to forge ahead. Or maybe our friend was moved by an inspirational novel loaned him by an acquaintance about a man who, against great odds, crafted a life of stability and contentment.

Whatever those positive events were, let's assume our our friend took them to heart and finally *changed his mind* about his victim status. He decided enough was enough. He thought new thoughts instead of replaying the old ones, and those thoughts were dutifully fed inward. His inner self picked them up—we will assume with joy at this long-overdue turn of events—and easily created a different set of probabilities for our friend. Then, miracle of miracles, our victim's circumstances started to alter.

And that takes us back to the two characteristics of Framework 2 mentioned above. There were no impediments in Framework 2 which would have prevented our man from shucking his victim status; indeed, Framework 2 leaned in his favor in order to make it happen.

Framework 1, or physical life, is usually approached with a belief in cause and effect; that is, you do something to me (cause), and I feel something and respond to you (effect). Basically, this classical definition of cause and effect says I am impacted by your actions. That's okay as long as I view your actions as "good," but if that's not the case and I believe you're hurting me in some way, I will react accordingly, possibly through aggression or anger, or maybe as a silent victim. But however I react, you can bet I'll think of you as the initiator of my problems.

What really happens is exceedingly different than that old-line thinking suggests. As we now know, when we feel a certain way or believe a certain thing, that information is fed into Framework 2. An event is selected from the field of probabilities based on our input, and in it comes to physical reality to be experienced. So then what, we might ask? What is next on the docket? Well, how we *respond* to the event emotionally and intellectually is fed into Framework 2, another event is chosen based on our feelings and thoughts, and that event comes in to be experienced. Ad infinitum.

So, what happened to cause and effect? It's still there, but now it takes on a whole new meaning. We *cause* the events we face in life; events portray the *results* of our thinking. Cause and effect in the classical sense dies a well-deserved death, but cause and effect in the psychical sense remains alive and well. And that means we must assume we are the architects of all the experiences we meet in this reality, from our ultra-successes to the minor "coincidences" sprinkled throughout our days. As Seth tells us, "The coincidences that seem to happen, the chance encounters, the unexpected events—all of these come into your experience because in one way or another you have attracted them, even though their occurrences might seem to have insurmountable odds against them. Those odds—those impediments—do not exist in Framework 2."[10]

Irene's Event

An event is as creative a production as, say, painting a picture or writing a poem. While a picture comes to life on canvas, and poetry on paper, an event is impressed on time and space. The event becomes the medium for expression, and the people involved become the living embodiment of the ideas at play. An event is a living "peoplescape" in which each person joins the creative act, and becomes the creative act.

Our individual realities exist more in Framework 2 than Framework 1, so says Seth. That's where the main action takes place. That's where a creative idea buds; that's where decisions beyond number take place and where infinite computations must occur in order to bring that idea to fruition and then integrate it into the exterior world; and that's where all the alignments are made with the people who will take the creative idea and run with it in physical reality.

For instance, the idea for a new song pops into Irene's head one fine day. She goes about writing the lyrics and composing the tune. When it's completed, she cuts a demo tape and finds herself an agent. The agent eventually lines up a deal with a recording company, the contracts are signed and Irene sings her way into the hearts of millions.

What actually happened in this scenario? Framework 2 furnished Irene with a creative idea, she felt the nudge to listen to this impulsive information, and so latched on to the idea and called it her own. With strong interaction and assistance from Framework 2, she developed the idea into its final form—a finished song. Meanwhile, a set of probabilities coalesced in Framework 2 that would support infinite possibilities around Irene's song, some more probable than others based on Irene's intent and beliefs.

In Framework 2, where each person is connected to every other person, mental communication was initiated that led Irene and her agent-to-be to meet in the dream state and devise a plan in which they would meet in physical reality again. The agent was primed to accept Irene as a client, but Irene could have blown it in daily life by wavering in her beliefs. Had she become uncertain, fearful, depressed, or any number of other things, her feelings could have altered her intent, which then would have altered the outcome of being accepted by the agent. But in our scenario, we will assume Irene held her belief in herself and her work strongly, thereby allowing the agent to move ahead with Plan A.

Time goes by in Framework 1 while Irene anxiously awaits word from her agent that a potential deal has been identified. Other events not associated with the song scenario happen to both the agent and Irene throughout their days, and some of those events may throw one or both off track for a period of time. Static, Seth calls it, static at the Framework 1 level that has the potential of impacting Framework 2.

However, Irene's intent is still strong; that is, she hasn't lost faith in herself or her ability to make her song a success, and the agent's intent, while not at Irene's level, still places a good amount of focus on Irene's project. The result: Irene and her agent meet up with a recording company executive in Framework 2, and they rehearse a scene bound for Framework 1 in which all parties agree to sign a contract. No one changes his or her mind later in Framework 1, and so the event comes to pass.

Again, though, before the final scene is played out over lunch with the flourish of a pen on the contract's dotted line, much has happened in each player's private life. Conflicts, resolutions, love, resentments, happiness, anxiety...the stuff of life as it is played out in daily living color. Those events, while they seem isolated from the present scene in the restaurant, are not. They reflect, in many ways, the same values that are brought to the table along with the contract.

In other words, resentments that fester toward the neighbor who placed a fence one inch over the border on to the property of the agent may symbolize his feelings of being constricted or pushed by outside sources. Those feelings may then continue during—and color—his dealings with the record company. Static. Static in Framework 1 which can impact the strength of the deal being honed over Caesar Salad.

And what if the feeling brought to the table is instead one of simple regard and trust, simple regard for each consciousness who has agreed to participate in the present event and trust in a supportive universe which will fulfill the needs and desires of all involved? It's self-evident. That's not to say harps will sound in the background and auras of love will surround the group. Indeed, the successful conclusion to the signing of the contract may even seem to snag. Intermittent static from one of the group, possibly, but not the end of the story. Irene wants her song recorded for her own reasons, the agent wants the song recorded for his own reasons, the recording company wants some song recorded that will become a hit, and its staff members on the negotiation team have their own personal reasons for being involved.

If this combined group's desires are firmly held at the Framework 2 level and they can bypass the Framework 1 static (or at least deal with it), they can meet in ordinary life the results of their desires as decided upon in Framework 2.

And if they don't wrap up the loose ends of limiting emotions and beliefs over lunch, they could go their separate ways and create other events in Framework 2 that will lead each of them to their individual goals, possibly involving a whole new group of people.

But let's assume this original group works it out and accepts the first Framework 2 possible event as their own. The big event doesn't end with the signing of the contract. Don't forget the millions who reach out to Irene's song and make it gold. They, also, agree to play parts in the unfolding of the action. They have needs and desires that are met by their appreciation of Irene's work. Irene's intent in Framework 2 is the primary mover in this scenario, so if she stays clear on her desire and sees her work as valuable, the people who will come to appreciate it in Framework 1 will join together to "finish" the event for Irene.

Every event is the result of multidimensional creativity. All of the people involved are in it for their own reasons and purposes, and none can be manipulated to suit the needs and desires of anyone else. No one is a pawn in someone else's game of life. Emotional intensity drives an event to fruition; without it there is no force and vitality to keep it developing or evolving in Framework 2. Each player holds his or her own level of intensity, depending on the importance of the outcome of the event in their lives. To Irene, getting her song recorded was of primary emotional focus, so the nucleus of probabilities which formed in Framework 2 centered around Irene's vigorously held desire.

The agent and negotiating team were willing players, cooperating with Irene because her desire brought something to their own personal parties, but their focus could not be called vigorous. On the other hand, Irene was playing a bit part in *their* private dramas, dramas which may have had little to do with the success or failure of Irene's single song, but everything to do with some other multi-layered goal of their own. Irene entered their realities based on what they wanted to experience; they weren't simply supporting cast members to her prima donna role. No players would have been a part of the event unless their thoughts, attitudes, beliefs, intents and focus had not drawn them to it. They did not agree to participate for no reason at all; there is always an underlying personal reason for anyone to enter an event.

Our minds form events and material objects so adroitly—and automatically—that we seldom spot the creative act in progress. However, when we *purposefully* form an intent via thought or imagination, apply the paintbrush of desire, and have faith it will come into being, we start to sense the great power of the mind, because we will eventually see the objectified results of our focus.

Static Interference

Where do we want to focus our energy, Framework 1 or Framework 2? This is a very important question, because the answer spells the difference between constantly butting our heads against the wall and flowing with life. Let's say our desire is to enjoy a leisurely walk one summer evening down to the neighborhood ice cream parlor. We're half way there when a car roars by just as we enter the crosswalk. Stupid driver, we think, he could have hit me. We mull the incident over in our mind, with a couple expletives thrown in for good measure.

About then some kids whiz by on skateboards, virtually forcing us off the sidewalk and onto the adjoining grass. Now we're really getting hot under the collar. Damn kids never show responsibility nowadays. We mull the incident over in our mind, with a couple expletives thrown in for good measure. When we reach the ice cream parlor, it's bursting with customers. Looks like a long wait, we grouse.

This evening isn't exactly turning into what I desired when I left home, we think as we adjust to the loud noise and interminable wait.

Well, no it isn't. By reacting to static in Framework 1, we re-selected probabilities in Framework 2. We mitigated our intent in Framework 2 for a pleasant evening by allowing our thoughts to develop a different intent from that of the original one. As our crankiness grew, our intent shifted to the creation of an event that would reflect the discoloration of irritation. Yes, we got our ice cream that evening, but the result of our goal left something to be desired.

And the questions that beg attention are these: When did the kids on the skateboard get selected as an event we'd meet in time and space? Was it when we started to harbor ill will toward the car's driver? Did the ice cream parlor become packed before or after we became upset at the skateboard kids? How would the events of the evening have turned out if we'd *bypassed the static of Framework 1* and let Framework 2 work for us?

This is a simple example, but nonetheless telling, about how life unfolds much of the time. We place a clean, clear wish into Framework 2 and then many times run it off course because of our static in Framework 1. Sometimes that self-generated static will kill the possibility of the wish being fulfilled completely, and at other times the event will become a watered down version of what it could have been—in the form of less money than we desire, a very slow recovery from an illness, a relationship that is okay but not wonderful, a new car that needs immediate repairs.

We initiate static into Framework 1 in other ways, also. One of the more common, for many of us, is through our belief that we won't reach our goal if we don't "work" Framework 1 to death. Since we believe Framework 1 is the sole source of our power, we pressure ourselves into situations that could better be handled through a joint effort expended between the two frameworks.

Let's say you are a product manager ready to launch a new product, and since you don't believe in Framework 2, you expend all your effort in Framework 1. You have been taught to initiate a great amount of details as part of any product release, so you prepare data sheets, news releases, mailings, advertisements, publicity, etc.

You attend unending staff and executive meetings and focal groups where all bases are noted and covered, where all ideas are explored in depth. You do all the right things, according to the book of Hoyle, and you become stressed out with the pressure of trying to create a winner, anxious about the competition and concerned about the future. Late night work and Rolaids become more commonplace as the product is prepared for first deliveries.

The problem is you assume the success of the product, and yours as a manager, is decided by what you do in Framework 1. Not so, according to Seth in an unpublished session dated November 21, 1979. "When you concentrate <u>mainly</u> in Framework 1...there are glaring discrepancies: entanglements that you do not like because you have taken your intent from Framework 2, where the creative event began, and placed it into Framework 1's communication system almost entirely. Obviously you need Framework 1, with its letters, telephone calls, and so forth, but Framework 1's communication system, while physically handy, also is somewhat like a very poor telephone connection, with static at both ends.

"You reach each person you want separately. You must make your message clear regardless of the other person's needs or circumstances, intents of the moment, and so forth. The more harassed you become, the more the static increases at both ends.

"Now: Framework 2's communication system is set into motion as a primary rather than as a backup system of communications...(It) is at once simpler and more complex than Framework 1's...Your clear intent is communicated to each of the people involved—at a <u>level</u> without static—yours or theirs. You set a far more favorable group of probabilities into motion, a group that aids you and them as well, for they are also seeking creativity from their separate viewpoints. They are also fighting their own static. You do not have to contact them one by one in Framework 2. The (project) itself is like a magnet..."

Later in the same session, Seth says, "To brood or worry, or become resentful is as regrettable as it would be if you, say, painted a big X over one of your paintings because you were dissatisfied with a detail or two. Over a period of time, resentments X out large areas of otherwise productive experience....When you have fearful thoughts about a (project), then you feed other people's static. You increase to some extent their doubts as well as your own."

Okay, so how do we deal with the static in Framework 1? How do we respond to people who irritate us, situations which upset us, circumstances which impact us? We drop our negative feelings toward them. We fall into an at-ease position, and literally change our minds about how we will react. We relax. We clear our minds. We remember that there are infinite probabilities at our disposal, so we decide to loosen up and let Framework 2 plop one of its goodies into our lap, instead of our causing more static through our thoughts. We stop hammering Framework 1 with the cry of "Results, please!" and instead follow the impulses and intuitive nudges from Framework 2 that will lead us to the fulfillment of our desire.

And remember that we're always working with the big picture of our desire and intent. If an event goes against your liking, keep in mind that it is only one step on the walk to your goal. Don't worry about it. One sour event, or even several, is not indicative of a goal out of reach or stymied. Just because you don't fill the house for your first public violin performance doesn't mean you won't become the well-known musician you desire to be. So you don't score 100 each and every time. So what? It's all part of the process, so relax with it.

Changing the Party Line

Consciousness is given the greatest gift of all—it gets exactly what it wants. From nothing we weave the web of magical experiences. Our joys and accomplishments, our tortures and desperation are all part of our own energy, literally. How we handle these self-created events is up to our individual natures and is based on free will. But eventually we must understand that we are learning to be conscious creators of our realities.

Such knowledge doesn't come without a price tag, however, for once we understand our enormous power of creation, we must eventually own up to the responsibility attached to it. Eventually we're supposed to understand that we're creating it all by focusing tremendous amounts of energy in certain directions based on what's held in our minds. So, the next logical step is to assess our creations and determine if they are to the good of ourselves, our families, our communities, our civilization and nature. And if any part of the answer is no, we've got work to do.

As Seth tells us, "Despite all appearances, conditions of an exterior nature do not cause wars, or poverty, or disease, or any of the unfortunate circumstances apparent in the world. Your beliefs form your reality. Your thoughts generate practical experience. When these change, conditions will change."[11] And so it is we must change. It's up to us to do it with verve and vigor, keeping our conscious minds clear to the tones of deeper knowledge that surge from the vaster portions of ourselves, allowing our inner selves to form splendid symbolic expressions in our private and global worlds.

6

You are not a forsaken offshoot of physical matter, nor is your conscious-ness meant to vanish like a puff of smoke. Instead, you form the physical body that you know at a deeply unconscious level with great discrimina-tion, miraculous clarity, and intimate unconscious knowledge of each minute cell that composes it. This is not meant symbolically.

—*Seth*, Seth Speaks, *Session 512*

The Inside Out Phenomenon

Perhaps the most misguided belief held by much of the world's population is that the body is a separate entity, tied to nothing and obvious in its detachment. Most of us see our body as physically disconnected from nature and other liv-ing forms, with an unquestionable buffer of space between us and them. The closest we come to believing in any kind of a direct connection is an interface with the mind, and even that is limited in many ways by our thinking. The true story is so astounding, however, that a simple belief in a mind-body connection seems almost primitive by comparison. Seth says, "Your scientists are finally learning what philoso-phers have known for centuries—that mind can influence matter. They still have to discover the fact that mind <u>creates</u> and forms matter."[1]

We live in a sea of consciousness units. Physical reality is contained within this sea of consciousness. Nothing is apart from it, not the air we breathe nor the hangnail on our index finger. And this oneness of all things, this literal wholeness within the sea of consciousness, comes with a built-in communication system. Consciousness units communicate constantly and instantaneously with each other. This means that no matter what form certain CUs have chosen to experience, from tree to human, they are in communication with all other CUs.

Great amounts of information pass between all aspects of nature this way. It jumps from species to species and human organ to human organ, and much of it happens at the cellular level. Seth says, "Cellular transmission, for example, is indeed much more precise than any verbal language, communicating data so intricate that all of your languages together would fall far short of matching such complexity. This kind of communication carries information that a thousand alphabets could not translate. In such a way, one part of the body knows what is happening in every other part, and the body as a whole knows its precise position on the surface of the planet. It is biologically aware of all the other life-forms around it to the most minute denominator."[2]

The information the cells transmit to each other comes to them from Framework 2, the place where the intricate webwork of possibilities is developed and future probabilities created. The cells pick up the information and then go about the business of evolving the matter of which they are a part into what the future probabilities suggest. For instance, if the world consciousness makes the decision in Framework 2 to experience an epidemic, all cells in all forms of matter know of the decision immediately. And if it is the intent of a given personality gestalt (i.e., person) to be part of the epidemic, it prepares itself for the future event. When the epidemic "hits," the body is ready to be impacted. And on a more localized level, if a personality gestalt decides it will experience a sore neck, it will organize the body's system to react accordingly.

The biggest breakthrough that will allow us to live natural, healthy lives will occur when we understand the great purpose behind how and why our consciousness uses the body as a tool for expression, and the way all cells in the body work in concert through constant communication to bring about specific results based on what consciousness wants to experience. Basically, that's the stuff of this chapter. So, fasten your psychic seat belts and prepare for a ride through the hills and valleys of consciousness, on a road that leads from the inside out.

Settling in to Form

Nothing is by chance in our reality—nothing. If it's here as an event or a thing, then consciousness *decided* to put it into place. Indeed, consciousness chose to put the whole of physical reality into place for various reasons. One was that a certain kind of consciousness desired specific developments within itself, and it decided a solution was a physical reality where it could experience a long-term identification with form.

When consciousness first created our reality and populated it with itself playing the roles of air, nature, people, animals and all other matter, its attachment to the forms it became a part of was fluid. It would play at maintaining its physical structure for awhile, and then pull out for periods of time and explore the reality as free, unformed energy, eventually ending up back in its "solid" state. For instance, consciousness conducting life as a human would temporarily leave the body to function at a much reduced level of maintenance while it went off and did other things. As time went on, however, it became apparent that consciousness in the physical world would have to "forget" its ability to flit in and out of form if it expected to learn all it desired about physical manipulation in a reality driven by thought. So, it decided to fiercely identify, as Seth terms it, with the body, and stay put during waking hours.

The upshot was that consciousness came to view the body as primary, instead of as a secondary energy construction, and at the same time it lost touch with the fact that, not only the body, but *everything* in physical reality is simply consciousness taking on form. It got turned around in its thinking and came to believe the psychic or psychological constructions it created and then experienced were solely earthly constructions, and started reacting to them as such. That mind set, solidified by the development of the ego, is what led the human race to believe it stands alone in the world, detached and vulnerable. According to Seth, we've taken the idea of separateness as far as we can without causing greater pain and anguish, so it's time once again to remember who and what we really are, and to change our behavior to match our heritage. Seth says his purpose is to open our eyes.

So, we must start with the premise that everything we see and experience is consciousness under development. Then the rest of what we'll discuss falls into place naturally.

Inside Evolution

Not surprisingly, the history of the body doesn't start with birth. There is an infinite amount of planning that goes into the body's structure before it becomes physical, and some of it is rather intriguing. For instance, our information source says, "Each inner self, adopting a new body, imposes upon it and upon its entire genetic makeup, memory of the past physical forms in which it has been involved. Now the present characteristics usually overshadow the past ones. They are dominant, but the other characteristics are latent and present, built into the pattern. The physical pattern of the present body, therefore, is a genetic memory of the self's past physical forms, and of their strengths and weaknesses."[3]

But while the body's genetic makeup is influenced by the "past," its growth is directly related to the future. The concept of evolution says there is a progression of physical development and change over a given time line, moving the species from the past into the present. Not so, according to Seth. True evolution happens in Framework 2 and is based on what the species expects to see in the *future*. Those expectations become part of what seems to be an evolutionary change in Framework 1. But the direction toward change happens outside physical reality first, and is in direct response to a future time seen and sensed by consciousness in physical form. As Seth says, "...Evolution does not march from the past into the future. Instead, the species is precognitively aware of those changes it wants to make, and from the 'future' it alters the 'present' state of the chromosomes and genes to bring about in the probable future the specific changes it desires."[4] The energy of All That Is goes outward as consciousness, forming manifestations of itself throughout time as vital and alive as it is. Each species is precognitively aware at the cellular level of the changes it wants to make, and it goes about setting the future stage for thdse changes via the genes and chromosomes.

There is no such thing as classical evolution, per se, under these guidelines. Complex physical forms do not evolve from simpler ones, although it does take a more complicated consciousness organization to create and become that type of physical structure. Consciousness joins groupings in Framework 2 based on what it wants to experience—the complexity of the creature that eventually emerges from Framework

2 will not have evolved to its present state because of an earthly linear time frame. Of Charles Darwin and his theory of evolution, Seth says, "He spent his last years proving it, and yet it has no real validity. It has a validity within very limited perspectives only; for consciousness does, indeed, evolve form. Form does not evolve consciousness...The theory of evolution is as beautiful a tale as the theory of Biblical creation."[5]

Consciousness Choosing Conditions

Heredity takes on a different meaning under the banner of this information, also. One issue is that, as mentioned, consciousness forms the genes, and this means consciousness chooses its supposed heredity to suit its purposes. Says our inside source: "In simple terms, you choose ahead of time the kind of body you will inhabit...The genes and chromosomes do not just happen to have within them the precisely defined coded information that will be needed. The data is impressed upon them from within. The identity exists before the form. You could say that the identity, existing in another dimension entirely, plants the seed into the medium of physical reality from which its own material existence will spring."[6]

Consciousness can alter its cellular structure when and if it suits its purposes. Whatever changes consciousness decides to make are possible because of the fact that time is not linear. To clarify this point, here's Seth: "Basically, cellular comprehension straddles time. There is, then, a way of introducing 'new' genetic information to a so-called damaged cell in the present. This involves the manipulation of consciousness, not gadgets, as well as the use of a time-reversal principle. First the undesirable information must be erased. It must be erased in the 'past' in your terms...The body on its own performs this service often, when it automatically rights certain conditions, even though they were genetically imprinted. The imprints become regressive. In your terms, they fade into a probable series of events that do not physically affect you."[7]

Because we experience a linear world, with what we believe is a concrete past and unknown future, our scientific theories are honed from that assumption. The assumption is never questioned. We presume our world is pushed forward by the past, kicking and screaming itself into a future that in many ways mirrors the past in spite of major scientific breakthroughs. For instance, some diseases are eliminated, yet others seem to raise their heads and ask to be experienced. Why? Because we *believe* in our vulnerability to disease and illness, we keep manifesting them quite nicely. Our belief is projected into the future via our thoughts—meaning we expect to meet it some day—and, by golly, there it is, waving at us from some future date. Seth says, "Your body's condition at any time is not so much the result of its own comprehension of its 'past history' as it is the result of its own comprehension of future probabilities. The cells precognate."[8] The future pulls us to it based on what we expect to see. What do we want that future to reflect?

Patterns From Inside

As we're told in *The Individual and the Nature of Mass Events*, "You observe a table's surface as smooth and solid, even though you realize it is composed of atoms and molecules full of motion. In the same way you experience a birthday party, an automobile accident, a bridge game, or any psychological event as psychologically solid, with a smooth experienced surface that holds together in space and time. Such events, however, consist of invisible 'particles' and faster-than-light perceptions that never show. In other words, they contain psychic components that flow from

Framework 2 into Framework 1."[9]

The key to understanding our body is the same as understanding the genesis of an event, because the body is an ongoing event. It flows, newly formed, from Framework 2 into Framework 1 moment by moment. The fantastic energy of our inner self, or our greater psyche, creates our physical body and maintains it, constantly. That energy emerges into physical reality as continual pulsations, meaning the body actually blinks on and off. Seth says we are not "here" equally as often as we are here. "For every moment of time that you seem to exist in this universe, you do not exist in it. The atoms and molecules have a pulsating nature that you do not usually perceive, so what seems to you to be a continuous atom or molecule is, instead, a series of pulsations that you cannot keep track of."[10]

Matter, including the human form, is not permanent. Like our consciousness, it flashes in and out of Framework 1, fueled from Framework 2. Basically, our body constantly emerges from the field of probabilities, entering the now point of our experience. Its integrity holds from one pulsation to the next because of the body's pattern that is impressed on Framework 2. Indeed, our body *could not exist* if there was not a corresponding pattern found outside time and space. Its fleshy form is obvious in Framework 1, yet that form is a projection into our three-dimensional field from our much greater reality.

The magic of the universe assures us that our body will always be there for us, that it will seem stabilized in time with us centered snugly within it. The specialized selectivity that earth-tuned consciousness uses to create its reality from a myriad of unseen choices also allows our consciousness to jump over the unrecognized lapses in form. But the fact is that our body fluctuates in and out of time and space constantly, and with each fluctuation comes ongoing change.

Seth says, "The physical matter that composed your body a moment ago is different in important ways from the matter that forms your body this instant. If you perceived the constant change within your body...then you would be amazed that you ever considered the body as one more or less constant, more or less <u>cohesive</u>, entity."[11]

Our body changes completely every seven years, according to Seth, yet with each immediate breath we take, many significant changes occur. For instance, he says that atoms and molecules die and are replaced, hormones are altered, and "electromagnetic properties of skin and cell continually leap and change, and even reverse themselves." On one level of self we know each minute alteration that happens to our body, but because we strive to maintain a permanent-seeming environment, we ignore them. But the reality is we grow our body moment by moment, using the building blocks of atoms and molecules to create an intimate form we call our own.

Since we live in a physical system, we must have a physical body, because only the physical senses, via the brain, can translate the information residing in Framework 2 into workable models in Framework 1. In *The Nature of the Psyche*, Seth describes the brain's function as follows: "The brain is primarily an event-forming psycho-mechanism through which consciousness operates." So, to experience this reality demands we have a brain, which dictates we have a body. But while a physical body is a must, it is still the secondary construct to what is first developed in Framework 2. The body's integrity is intimately tied to that invisible pattern in the inner world. The invisible counterpart to the body that resides in Framework 2 isn't detached from our physical form or tissue, or separate in any way. And this point becomes very important when trying to understand how healing occurs, because however the pattern in Framework 2 goes, so goes our body. Our nonphysical pattern happens first; the body reflects the pattern.

And from where does Framework 2 get the data that tells the cells what alterations are appropriate in order to match the inner pattern? Where else? From our thoughts, attitudes, beliefs, feelings, intent and focus. Our body's condition perfectly mirrors our subjective state at any given time. Our Framework 2 body pattern responds quickly and accurately to what the mind is thinking; it responds to our conscious mental acts. What we think and believe is fed into Framework 2, the body pattern is altered accordingly, and the physical body then precisely mirrors its nonphysical counterpart. As we're told by Seth, "Within the basic framework of the body chosen before physical birth...the individual has full freedom to create a perfectly healthy functioning form. The form is, however, a mirror of beliefs, and will accurately materialize in flesh those ideas held by the conscious mind. That is one of the body's primary functions. A sick body is performing that function then, in its way, as well as a healthy one. It is your most intimate feedback system, changing with your thought and experience, giving you in flesh the physical counterpart of your thought."[12]

Our body is healthy or not healthy because of our conscious thoughts and intents. We literally affect its structure, using whatever means we will allow to make it ill or strong. If we believe in Western medicine, have faith in its power and agree to its authority, we'll visit a doctor, get our pills, and perhaps feel secure enough to allow healing to occur. If we believe in alternative medicine, the same result can happen. And if we believe we don't need any help in healing, that we can do it alone, the same result can happen. "You can cause a cell, or a group of cells, to change their self-image, for example; and again, you do this often—as you healed yourselves of diseases because of your intent to become well. The intent will be conscious, though the means may not be."[13]

So, what thoughts and intents cause illness? It depends on what being sick buys us personally. For instance, we might use it to achieve failure or success. Pride or humility. Renown or oblivion. Honor or dishonor. The question to ask our self if we become ill is, what do I gain from this? Does it catapult me into feeling loved or disliked? Courageous or cowardly? Significant or insignificant? Whatever our answer, you can bet we chose the illness to fit our needs of the day.

Heredity falls into the category of "use if needed," also. Our *belief* in a hereditary condition or propensity can actually activate the problem until finally its results become pronounced and verifiable. According to Seth, "There are obviously some conditions that in your terms are inherited, showing themselves almost instantly after birth, but these are of a very limited number in proportion to those diseases you believe are hereditary—many cancers, heart problems, arthritic or rheumatoid disorders. And in many cases of inherited difficulties, changes could be effected for the better, through the utilization of other mental methods..."[14]

Intrinsic to the body are abilities beyond our comprehension, at least based on what we accept as possible today. Seth says that many organs can replace themselves, and that diseased tissue can be eliminated and regenerated. He maintains that without realizing it many people who develop cancer but have not yet "verified" it openly, cure themselves of it; and that appendixes have grown back after surgery. And he also maintains that such powers of the body are "biologically quite achievable," if only we change our beliefs and intent.

The body is very capable of keeping itself in excellent health throughout its youthful years and far into old age, with only a gradual change occurring. It is built to maintain itself as a healthy long-living organism far beyond our present understanding. It is also well equipped to reach the highest levels of physical achievements, and to rid itself of any disease or illness. In other words, the body's pattern in Framework 2 holds all the probabilities for creating and maintaining the physical form in its ultimate condition. And as usual our inner self plays an integral role: "You may ...unknowingly acquire an illness and recover, never aware of your malady, being healed because of a series of events that would seemingly have nothing to do with the illness itself—because in Framework 2 the inner (self) knowing both the reason for the illness, and its cure, brought about those precise situations that remedied the condition. Such events happen automatically, when nothing hampers recovery at your end."[15]

When nothing hampers recovery at our end? Now what might Seth be referring to? Certainly our thoughts, attitudes and beliefs, but what about that secret ingredient discussed in chapter 3, the divine glue that holds the universe together—that little ol' thing called faith? William James says, "(Faith's) action in the body promotes exactly those biological changes necessary to ensure health and vitality so that the pulses may be quickened or slowed, the hormones activated or quieted. Faith elicits the most specific biological responses by inciting a general overall sense of optimism, safety, and freedom. It therefore returns the individual, for whatever time, to that prime condition for growth..."[16]

Physical Reality's Continuum

We could not maintain a physical reality, including a body, without there being another dimension of activity, a deeper area of the psyche, where our life is developed with a wisdom and knowledge lacking in conscious awareness.

This deeper area is an extension of our self, not a foreign realm with which we have little in common. Indeed, it is the flip side of our consciousness. In usual terms it's called the sleep state. Seth says, "In sleep the conscious actually becomes the subconscious, and the subconscious in a very real manner, becomes conscious. Every man instinctively knows this, and yet every man stubbornly refuses to admit it. The part of you who dreams is the I as much as the part of you that operates in any other manner. The part of you who dreams is the part of you who breathes. And this part is certainly as legitimate, and actually more necessary to you as a whole unit, than the part that also plays Bridge or Scrabble."[17]

Far from being a shambling, scattered field of activity, the dream state is laced with logic. Seth says, in fact, that the dreaming intellect can put our computers to shame. The information we work with in that protected area of the psyche is what makes our world go 'round, personally and globally. Everything of import that happens in physical reality is dealt with there first, from private events to ones that impact our civilization. As Seth tells us, "Events obviously are not formed by your species alone, so that...there is a level of the dream state in which all earth-tuned consciousnesses of all species and degrees come together. From your standpoint this represents a deep state of unconscious creativity—at the cellular levels particularly—by which all cellular life communicates and forms a vital biological network that provides the very basis for any 'higher' experience at all. What you call dreaming is obviously dependent upon this cellular communication, which distributes the life force throughout the planet."[18]

Consciousness is as active in sleep as in the ordinary awake state—actually, even more so. Part of our consciousness leaves the body each night through "adjacent corridors" of reality, activating the higher centers of intuition that each of us possesses as it travels inward. The physically oriented portion of consciousness stays behind and maintains the body. The purpose of these nightly trips is well defined and very important. In what Seth terms the most protected area of sleep, deeper than the dream state and not traceable through brain patterns, we participate in two separate activities. One is a passive state in which we are given information to absorb and concepts to study. The other is considered active, since this is the state where we take what we learned that evening in the passive state and perceive it in new ways, especially through participation and examples. This state is also used to rejuvenate the body.

As we return to a less "distant" state of consciousness, the teachings we've explored are formed into dreams that will encompass the new information. Many times practical advice in specific areas has been given us, and in the dream state we replay the advice in the guise of translatable symbols. Then, in the awake state, we're fed the advice in final, practical form, so to speak. For instance, in regard to healing, Seth says, "In most cases the stimuli (toward healing) come from deeper levels of the self, where they may be translated into terms that the personal subconscious can use. In such cases, these perceptions may find their way to the ego, appearing as inspirations or intuitive thought."[19]

So, there is significant purpose to our nightly time-outs. Our body is rejuvenated, future events are analyzed and acted out, choices are discussed and decisions made. And, just as important, assistance is given that can lead us out of a blind alley of beliefs. Our inside contact tells us that, "Alternate paths of experience—new possibilities and intuitive solutions—constantly appear in the dream state, so that man's learning is not simply dependent upon a feedback system that does not allow for the insertion of creative material...There may be, for example, complications arising from a person's intents, loves, and desires that cause the individual to seek certain events that his or her very beliefs make impossible...In such instances a dream, or a series of them, will often then alter the person's beliefs in a way that could not otherwise occur, by providing new information."[20]

The dream state is, in many ways, our salvation. Thankfully our inner selves were wise enough to know how much assistance would be necessary once we made the transition from consciousness denying its roots to consciousness knowing its roots. If we'd been left to live out the conclusions drawn by our conscious minds alone, our race of earth-tuned consciousness would not have survived a decade, let alone untold centuries. We'd have annihilated nature and each other many moons ago, sadly locked into belief systems that left us nowhere to go except downhill. But, fortunately, we create our lives from the inside out, and part of that creation takes place in the dream state where fresh information, new understandings and solid advice are part of every night's activity.

Dying on Purpose

Death, portrayed as the great scary void, loses its fear factor the more we come to understand consciousness and its eternal, inviolate right to life. It's exceedingly apparent that there is no death, in the deepest sense. All there is is a change of focus by the consciousness which chooses to leave physical reality. But even the act of leaving is not something foreign to us, experienced just once per lifetime. Not only does our body "die" and become replenished many times during our years on earth, but our consciousness leaves our body every night, using the same corridor as during the "permanent" departure.

Seth says we project our consciousness out of our body

while in a portion of the sleep state, actually moving about our homes—or other people's—by using the inner senses that come as standard operating equipment for all consciousness, anywhere. We leave our body in the capable hands of our body consciousness while our main consciousness focuses on other things for awhile. Part of the purpose of our nightly foray is to learn how to move our consciousness around through thought, without a body to slow us down. And part of the reason for that exercise is so we'll feel comfortable with not having a body once we die. According to Seth, the after-death environment is simply one in which "different laws apply, and the laws are far less limiting than the physical ones with which you now operate. In other words, you must learn to understand and use new freedoms."[21] And it seems we start practicing our after-death freedoms while still alive.

But why is there a thing called death at all? Why must we die? Basically, Seth says the self outgrows the flesh, that the "exuberant, ever-renewed energies of the spirit can no longer be translated into flesh." The self experiences what it desires in a given lifetime, and then makes the decision to go on to other experiences. So the decision is made to depart the body. "There is a time when you, as a consciousness, decide that death will happen, when in your terms you no longer bridge the gap of minute deaths not accepted. Here consciousness decides to leave the flesh, to accept an official death."[22]

Is Seth saying we always choose our own deaths, without exception? Oh, yes. "Each person born desires to be born. He dies when that desire no longer operates. No epidemic or illness or natural disaster—or stray bullet from a murderer's gun—will kill a person who does not want to die."[23]

What consciousness in physical form hasn't seemed to learn yet is that death can be easy. Again, to quote our unusual source, "Ideally this desire for death, however, would simply involve the slowing of the body's processes, the gradual disentanglement of psyche from flesh; or in other instances, according to individual characteristics, a sudden, natural stopping of the body's processes. Left alone, the self and the body are so entwined that the separation would be smooth. The body would automatically follow the wishes of the inner self."[24]

Some people can lessen or eliminate their fear of death simply by accepting what Seth and others say about the impossibility of annihilation. Others can't. There is one foolproof way to overcome death-related anxiety, though. Teach yourself to consciously project your consciousness out of your body. Many people have trained themselves to do just that on a regular basis. My friend Mary Barton has written a book called *Soul Sight* in which she chronicles her story of over 350 out-of-body projections. Mary, and people like her, are leading the way toward a major world shift in understanding the fluidity, and eternal nature, of consciousness, and that understanding will irrevocably alter our definitions of life and death. Some day we will accept that, "The projection in time and space may disappear…wither and die. The main identity continues to exist…"[25]

But until then it helps to have one who has been there tell us what we don't yet know, and as usual Seth brings the subject nicely into perspective: "When one has been born and has died many times, expecting extinction with each death, and when this experience is followed by the realization that existence still continues, then a sense of the divine comedy enters in…All of my deaths would have been adventures had I realized what I know now. On the one hand you take life too seriously, and on the other, you do not take playful existence seriously enough."[26]

Joyful Implications

Whatever anyone thinks to the contrary, our bodies, indeed our realities, spring forth into actualization in each moment of time. It has only been through our stubborn insistence that we are not a part of the natural contour of consciousness that such a truth has escaped our awareness. And yet our ability to live comfortable lives with no unusual concerns hinges on our understanding this truth. If knowledge can bring joy, then surely this chapter's final quote from Seth plants our feet firmly on words with implications that are truly life altering: "In the most basic of ways, the world is formed from the inside out..."[27]

Probabilities are an ever-present portion of your invisible psychological environment. You exist in the middle of a probable system of reality. It is not something apart from you. To some extent it is like a sea in which you have your present being. You are in it, and it is in you. From this field of probabilities you choose patterns of thought which you will weave into the physical matter of your universe.

—*Seth,* The Seth Material, *Chapter 18*

To Be or Not to Be... Is a Probability Selection

The great flexibility of physical reality, the flexibility that allows each of us to develop a life of conscious choice, is dependent on time as we know it being an illusion. We cannot be locked into a present which is based on actions from a past, and we cannot be forced into a future based on either past or present actions and still say we create our realities from the point of power called the present. It just doesn't wash. Time must be so flexible that our pasts, presents and futures are decided in the moment, and changeable in the next...and then we can accurately say we create our realities from the now. Seth says, "All in all...we are speaking of a constant creation, even though I must explain it in serial terms. We are discussing a model of the universe in which creation is continuous, spontaneously occurring everywhere, and everywhere simultaneously, in a kind of spacious present, from which all experiences with time emerge."[1]

As discussed previously, physical reality is actually a psychological medium decorated to look physical. To give the appearance of continuity, space and time were selected as root assumptions for the developing creative endeavor. But since space and time are props specifically designed for this stage set and have value only in a physical setting, they have no intrinsic duration. In other words, they don't influence us as much as we assume—we can work outside their parameters. They are simply camouflage and as such hold far less sway over us than we realize.

Take cause and effect, for instance. That concept is based on a belief in linear time, or successive moments. We bow down to it in this reality because it seems an accurate assessment of how life flows. Science and psychology pay homage through their complete acceptance of it, and use it as the basis for their theories and conclusions. And yet Seth says, "There is no cause and effect in the terms in which you understand the words. Nor is there a succession of moments that follow one after the other. And without a succession of moments following one after another you can see that the idea of cause and effect becomes meaningless. An action in the present cannot be caused by an action in the past, and neither action can be the cause of future action, in a basic reality where neither past nor future exists."[2]

If there are no successive moments, what causes the comfortable camouflage of linear time? It is *intensity* within the electrical system in which our reality is immersed (the electrical system was briefly mentioned in chapter 2). Seth says, "...Time is indeed an electrical impulse that grows by intensity, and not by moments. To speak of backward and forward is meaningless. There are only various electric pulsations of varying intensities; since strong intensities are natural results of weaker intensities, it would be meaningless to call one present and one past...When the pulsation is weak, you call it past. When it is strongest, you name it the present, and one that seems to you not yet as strong as present, you name future. For you make the divisions yourselves."[3]

What Seth is saying is that outside of time and space we assign an intensity to a probable event, and depending on the level of intensity we give it, it will become a past event, a present event, or a future one. As we change our strength of intensity, events shift around until a "new" event seems to be our present, an "old" event seems to be part of our past, and one around which we haven't developed enough intensity lurks in our future. Yet *all* of the chosen events are decided upon in the now, or spacious present...the only time there is.

(And what happens to the events *not* chosen to be manifested? According to Seth, "Any event of any kind that does not directly, immaculately intersect with your space-time continuum, does not happen, in your terms, but falls away. It becomes probable in your system but seeks its own 'level,' and becomes actualized as it falls into place in another reality whose 'coded sequence' fits its own."[4] In other words, all events live on, even if we don't select them for manifestation in our space continuum.)

The fascinating thing about simultaneous time is that it is never too late to replace a past event with one we would rather have experienced. Seth says we do it all the time, and we do it by *changing what we think and believe* in the present. Consider a contagious disease, for example. Let's say we're feeling vulnerable, depressed, sad, or whatever it would take for us to decide to experience such an illness. In a reality that believes in linear time, it would seem the cause of the disease happened in our past, i.e., we were exposed to the virus some time ago. However, Seth says throughout his books that this is not how we build reality—we build it from the present. Here is one quote that gives us insight as to how the process works: "A sudden contemporary belief in illness will actually reach back into the past, affecting the organism at that level, and inserting into the past experience of the cells the initiation of those biological events that will then seem to give birth to a present disease."[5] So, in essence, we change our past in order to experience the present of choice.

We should clap our hands and shout "Hooray!" at this news, because it is precisely because of the nature of simultaneous time—and by extrapolation, probabilities—that we can radically alter our life by choice. Probabilities and simultaneous time are inseparable, for one flows naturally into the other and each supports the functioning of the other. They are pieces of the same pie, and they are both sorely needed by consciousness in physical reality. Linear time offers no flexibility for the creation of our personal reality; only simultaneous time and probabilities unlock the secret to such a miraculous gift. For when we change our mind in the present, both the past and the future are adjusted in order to validate and reflect our new assumptions.

According to Seth, we are constantly provided with an unending source of probable events from past and future, and from this unending source we compose the events of our lives. In this synthesis of quotes from *The Nature of Personal Reality*, he says, "Since all events occur at once in actuality, there is little to be gained by saying that a past event causes a present one. Past experience <u>does not cause present experience</u>. You are forming past, present and future simultaneously...A new belief in the present can cause changes in the past. When you alter your beliefs today you also reprogram your past...By changing the past in your mind, now, in your present, you can change not only its nature but its effect, and not only upon yourself but others...As far as you are concerned, then, the present is your point of action, focus and power, and from that point of volition you form both your future and past."

Arriving From Somewhere Else

From each new moment a past is tentatively built and a future tentatively selected—tentatively, because either can be changed by us in the next instant. Our whole physical creation, called life in some quarters, fans out from the present moment. Seth tells us, "Underneath this recognized order of events...there is actually a vast field of ever-occurring action. These fields of probabilities are action sources for your reality."[6] From the simplest to the most complex action desired in Framework 1, if it is not in the field of probabilities it isn't possible to experience it. (But, fortunately for us, every action/event in all of its forms is available for expression in physical life.) What this means is that each separate moment we experience is first selected from the field of probabilities and then inserted into physical reality—*and therefore each moment we experience is literally new.* It must be, if it follows the previous one "out" of the spectrum of probabilities. No moment can simply be a continuation or a preordained flow from the previous one. Each stands alone, with its own validity.

The implications of this information are quite intriguing in many ways. Take matter, for instance. Given Seth's definition of probabilities, it means that nothing can be permanent enough to age—not our home, our body, nor the California Redwoods—as aging is defined by today's sciences. This quote from our nonphysical source helps bring the idea into better focus: "Matter is continually created, but no particular object is in itself continuous. There is not, for example, one physical object that deteriorates with age. There are instead continuous creations of psychic energy into a physical pattern that appears to hold a more or less rigid appearance...The actual material that seems to make up the object has completely disappeared many times, and the pattern has been completely filled again with new matter...Matter of itself, however, is no more continuous, no more given to growth or age than is, say, the color yellow."[7]

If each moment we experience is a fresh one projected into our reality from the field of probabilities, what then, one might ask, happens to our definition of motion? Just as with matter, we find a very different picture awaiting our understanding. When we decide to take action, such as walking to the window, a succession of probabilities are selected that match our desire, and in they come, brushed with the *faux* patina of motion. *Faux* because motion...well, motion is not. There is no such thing. Norman Friedman, in a quote from his remarkable book *Bridging Science and Spirit*, describes Seth's version of motion: "When matter 'moves,' it does so as a series of projections and injections that create the illusion of motion, just as lights along a string quickly flashing on and off in succession look like a single light moving through space."[8] And Seth describes motion in this way: "All motion is mental and psychological motion, and all mental and psychological motion has electrical reality. The inner self moves by changing or moving through intensities from your physical field. Each new psychological experience opens up a new pulsation intensity, and gives greater actuality within the electrical system. To move through intensities within the electrical system gives the result of moving through time within the physical system."[9]

When we decided to walk to the window in the example above, the potential events stored in the field of probabilities were scanned, and ones matching our desire were chosen. So they would make sense in linear time, they were laid out one by one in a specific sequence, and *voilà*, the illusion of motion was created. Time as we know it becomes an ordering parameter, then, for the events we choose to actualize from the field of probabilities. Events are held there until called into action under certain circumstances, and then they are funneled into their proper time placement in physical reality.

Well, almost always funneled into their proper placement. Seth says, "...There is no rigid placement of events. That placement is acquired. The uncoordinated child's senses, for example, may hear words that will be spoken tomorrow, while seeing the person who will speak them today. Focusing the senses in time and space is to some extent an acquired art, then—one that is of course necessary for precise physical manipulation."[10]

Forming the Illusion

Before we take a closer look at the nature of probabilities, there is one more idea that needs to be discussed. It was mentioned in chapter 5, but to truly grasp the power of probabilities, it must be understood: We each reside in our individual space continuum and never enter the space continuum of another.

Think of it this way. We are consciousness in permanent residence in psychological space and non-time. From this nonphysical environment we can create anything we desire, including the illusion of other realities. So, let's say we decide to play the game of physical life. It means we must prepare by setting up part of our psychological space to match the assumptions accepted under physical conditions, such as linear time and permanent matter. We call this environment our space continuum. Each consciousness "entering" physical reality does the same thing and communicates via telepathy with all other consciousnesses tuned to the same frequency, and agreements are made as to what the world and local scenes will reflect.

So, the stage is now set for whatever fun and games we

wish to play individually and share globally. But I still dwell in my private space continuum which I crafted from my personal psychological medium, and you dwell in yours. If you want to picture them as overlapping, creating one big happy picture of earth life, please do so. But know it's a fantasy that is only helpful as long as you don't buy it totally.

Here's why. If we believe we all reside in one reality instead of individual ones, it seems we are victims of life's whims, that we can be and are buffeted constantly by sources outside of our control. After all, if there is only one stage for all events and we are all on it at the same time, fate must play the role of creator of events. It's the only answer that makes sense. I can't command a parking place by focused intent if there is one stage, because there's no telling who might already be parked in my place of choice. And I can't determine through conscious desire what I want to do with my life because others may interfere, unknowingly or otherwise.

But I *can* command a parking place by intent, and I *can* design some future events. I've done both, and dozens of my friends have, also. If we understand we reside in our own space continuum, we can start to sense the tremendous flexibility of life in physical reality. We can see better that events start life as probabilities outside time and space and enter our individual space continuums when we've selected them through thought. Just because others in our immediate family contract the bubonic plague, it has no influence on us unless we bring it into our own space continuum. We can and will experience virtually whatever we wish, depending on the nature of our thoughts, attitudes, beliefs, focus and intent.

When we are trying to understand how probabilities contribute to the creation of physical reality and how they afford us the opportunity to craft our life through conscious choice, knowing we create from the secure position of our own space continuum becomes of paramount importance. And now that we know it, it's time to study probabilities—that most fascinating of subjects—in more depth. And there is a good reason to do so, according to Seth: "The consciousness that you know can indeed now emerge into even greater realization of itself, but not by obsessively defending its old position. Instead it must recognize its power as the director of probable action, and no longer inhibit its own greater capacities."[11]

Probabilities Understood

Probabilities. The term sounds theoretical, removed from the intimacy of everyday living. Surely probabilities are simply the results of mathematical equations, distant and cool. But no, they are a part of the living universe of ideas, vibrant with their own form of life. In fact, *our* life depends on them. Says Seth, "Your reality is like a shining platform, a surface resting upon probabilities. You follow these so unconsciously and beautifully, you swim through them so easily, that it does not occur to you to question your origin, or the medium in which your experience has its existence... Any focus point of physical life is caused by a merging of probabilities."[12]

Throughout his books Seth makes reference to probabilities. Some of his statements offer, by implication, the knowledge we need to take control of what at times feels like an out-of-our-control existence. I culled from the material the ideas that especially caught my attention, and then listed them in an order in which they somewhat build one upon the other. Hopefully this will help us better understand the absolute power of the mind in creating its reality, because it is only through *knowledge* that we will ever accept the significance behind this statement of Seth's: "You can change the picture of your life at any time if only you realize that it is simply the one portrait of yourself that you have created from an unlimited amount of probable ones."[13]

So, let's take a look at some of the more intriguing comments Seth has made regarding the nature of the field of probabilities.

"This probable field...is composed of thought images, not physically materialized in your terms, but vivid store-houses of energy."[14]

What makes our universe go 'round? Thought. Even the field of probabilities is woven of thought images. Thought has an intense energy behind it that we are but beginning to grasp, and an unparalleled role in the literal creation of our life. Seth says one emotion has more power than it takes to send a rocket to the moon—and behind every emotion is thought. Can we even attempt to imagine, then, what power must reside in the field of probabilities?

"You use probabilities like blocks to build events."[15]

An event is not composed of simply one probability. It is a synthesis of many. In other words, the event of a hypo-thetical woman running a stop sign and into a tree at the corner of Oak and Main Street at noon on May 17 was the result of numerous probabilities strung throughout linear time, until a certain overall scenario was actualized. But there was no one probability that encompassed the totality of the accident.

"The nature of any given probable action does not lead to any particular inevitable act."[16]

Each action the woman took that led to the accident was a stand-alone event. The actions were not deliberately linked together to lead to any specific conclusion. The fact that she drove a certain street to arrive at the corner of Oak and Main exactly at noon meant little in the scheme of things. The result the woman wanted to experience was what was important, and even that result was not assured until the "final" event entered her reality. Simply running the stop sign did not put the woman in the inevitable position of hitting the tree.

"Now all of these possible actions have a reality at that point. They are all capable of being actualized in physical terms. Before you make your decision, each of these probable actions are equally valid."[17]

Instead of hitting the tree, the woman could have run the stop sign and gained immediate control of her car, or she could have come within inches of the tree but not made contact. And if she'd hit the tree, she could have died. The point is that a myriad of probabilities were available at the point of running the stop sign.

None of the multitudinous "possible actions" in the accident example was the stronger candidate by nature of its basic composition, more likely to enter physical reality because it carried a power or dynamic the others lacked. It is true that some possibilities may have been imbued with more intensity in the field of probabilities due to the accident victim's mind set, but that intensity was hers to change at any time prior to the end result.

"The majority of events do not 'solidify' until the last moment in your terms."[18]

The free will of consciousness assures us that we can change our mind at any time and alter the potential outcome of an event. Therefore, we need that flexibility built into our interaction with the field of probabilities. Events can't be decided so far in advance that we don't have time to rethink our position. In the case of the accident, then, the outcome was not selected until the "last moment."

"Each event you form from any set of probabilities automatically gives rise to new probabilities."[19]

Assume the woman was dead set on having an accident that day. She could have made it happen *anywhere, at any time* from almost any grouping of probabilities. Say she breezed through the corner of Oak and Main without mishap, for some reason not selecting that scenario as the accident site. But obviously the accident potential was latent at that corner. Perhaps, though, she chose instead to take advantage of the probabilities available when she exited her cleaners a half hour later: She hit the gas pedal instead of the brake, and ran into a light post. The actions or events that led up to the woman's accident were not what made the accident occur, even though most people in today's world would argue the point. What made the accident a manifest event was the woman's final decision.

"At no time are events predestined. With every moment you change, and every action changes every other action. I am able to look from a different perspective, but still see only probabilities."[20]

The woman in the auto accident was not fated to experience the mishap, a prisoner walking to the gallows of predestination. When she left her home that May morning to run errands, she was not locked into a course of self-destruction. She could have had leanings in that direction, but the freedom to alter the potential outcome was inherent in every action she took. How could it not be, when she was surrounded by unlimited probabilities as each moment replaced the next? The same goes for world events as well as personal ones, of course. No event is forced upon us, ever, not even earth changes. No matter how many psychics predict a global occurrence of whatever sort, we simply don't have to buy it. In fact, our *belief* in a psychic's prediction at times leads us into the suggested outcome. And our *belief* that there is no way out of a private dilemma leads us into the assumed outcome.

It all gets down to moving through probabilities, and fortunately the logistics of it all are not something we must teach ourselves. Seth says, "Now, you move through probabilities in much the same way that you navigate in space. As you do not consciously bother with all of the calculations necessary in the process of walking down the street, so you also ignore the mechanisms that involve motion through probable realities. You manipulate through probabilities so smoothly, in fact, and with such finesse, that you seldom catch yourself in the act of changing your course from one probability to another."[21]

"There are in your terms unlimited probable future events for which you are now setting groundworks. The nature of the thoughts and feelings you originate sets a pattern."[22]

There's no getting around it—thoughts and feelings create. Our future possibilities are direct results of what we think today. What we hold in our mind now, around all sorts of issues, starts the formation of our future probabilities.

So, what *do* we think? About life, love, money, happiness, success, self? About death, hatred, poverty, depression, failure, self? What do we think about living in a safe universe, a killer world, a hopeless place, a dynamite reality? What are our feelings about illness, health, youth, age, competition, cooperation, self? It is crucial to our conscious development to know what we think and feel, to get a handle on our beliefs, our focus, our intent. Read *The Nature of Personal Reality* and you'll never again forget how important are your beliefs, thoughts and feelings. Seth says, "In a manner of speaking, each belief can be seen as a powerful station, pulling to it from fields of probabilities only those signals to which it is attuned, and blocking out all others."[23]

Thought is the doorway to life. We know by now the woman in the accident could have changed her mind at the last moment and not hit the tree. That was always an option. However, what if the woman's strong underlying belief was in victimhood? What if she had played out the belief for years, nurturing it through lack of understanding? Even though she could have stopped this one incident, she still would draw other events to her of a similar depressing nature until she got to the core of her thinking and altered it.

Now let's assume the woman did just that: She changed her long-standing belief around victimization. Would her life change overnight? There is always that possibility, but more than likely it would take "time" to see the complete results in her everyday experience. Seth says, "When you try to change your convictions in order to change your experience, you also have to first stop the momentum that you have already built up, so to speak...There is a steady, even flow in which conscious activity through the neurological structure brings about events, and a familiar pattern of reaction is established. When you alter these conscious beliefs through effort, then a period of time is necessary while the structure learns to adjust to the new preferred situation. If beliefs are changed overnight, comparatively less time is required."[24]

This does not mean, however, that reflections of change are not immediately experienced. They show up here and there, in the way people treat us, in the way we treat our self, in pleasant events and peaceful moments. And, if we build on these times we can expedite the overall process of change. How exactly to do this? By noting these special moments, first of all. We must give validity to the small changes through recognition, otherwise we simply won't see any forward progress. We'll think nothing is happening in Framework 2 that supports our desire, and we'll lose faith. Then we will feed that hopeless feeling into Framework 2, and the positive attitudes that preceded it will become watered down with new emotions.

The answer to almost everything is to live in the now in a stability of emotion. Don't let things get us down, don't let our resentments run wild, don't let our self see events through negative glasses. Remember that how we respond to life's experiences starts the selection of the next probability we will meet, and the next self we will become. Seth tells us, "You must realize that you are indeed a probable you. Your experience is the result of beliefs...Alter the beliefs and any probable self can, within certain limitations, be actualized."[25]

The Freedom of Conscious Choice

Probabilities have intrigued me since the first time I read of them in Seth's books. I decided that if I knew enough about their nature, I could teach myself to consciously select them at times. As the years progress I playfully experiment with probabilities a lot, and while I cannot even come close to calling myself an expert at conscious selection, I can say that I have learned a great deal—mostly about myself. I started this book with the story of a missing New York hotel room key. Before I made my decision as to how to handle the key situation, I thought about probabilities. I knew that many equally valid probabilities surrounded the potential outcome of that missing key, and that the "final" result was still in the field of probabilities awaiting my selection. So my first task became to decide how I felt about *myself*. That answer would give me a basis for making a decision. And since

I have a healthy sense of security in this reality, my decision came easily.

However, knowing one's self at the moment of conscious probability choice is not always so necessary. Simply rejecting a possible outcome works, also. In other words, a person who still questions her safety in New York could select the same probability as I did and make it work. If she refuses, absolutely refuses in the moment, to fall prey to ill fortune, that would become an operative conscious choice. Technically, she would actually change her belief in vulnerability, perhaps for that one incident only, but nonetheless the belief would change. And that change would allow the woman to exert her powerful right to choose what she wishes to experience at the now point of her existence. And if she made that same choice for security often enough, her ongoing belief in vulnerability would automatically loosen and drop away. How could it not, when she had defeated its usual outcome *consciously* several times? Surely she'd start to see her freedom to choose her beliefs, instead of unconsciously acquiescing to them.

Our Time Has Come

Probabilities are the direct result of the free will granted consciousness by All That Is. As Seth says, "Basically...the motion of any wave or particle or entity is unpredictable— freewheeling and undetermined. Your life structure is a result of that unpredictability. Your psychological structure is also...Consciousness, to be fully free, had to surprise himself, itself, herself, constantly, through freely granting itself its own freedom, or forever repeat itself."[26] You can see, then, why there is so much flexibility in the selection of events, why predetermination is not standard procedure, why an event is not solidified until the last minute.

Not that we don't slot certain events for possibility, but those probable actions are still part and parcel of the free will package. For instance, Seth says, "Each person's 'individual' life plan fits in somewhere with that of his or her contemporaries. Those plans are communicated one to the other, and probabilities instantly are set into motion in Framework 2. To some degree or another calculations are made so that, for instance, individual A will meet individual B at a marketplace 30 years later—if this fits in with the intents of both parties. There will be certain cornerstone encounters in each person's life that are set up as strong probabilities, or as plans to be grown into."[27] "If" is the key word in that quote. Consciousness is completely free to rethink its position at any time and to change probabilities quickly.

Do you sense the potential for global change as more becomes understood of probabilities and how to work with them consciously? This incredible information, and its practical implementation, can alter our race's thinking and move us into a whole new mode of conscious living, given a serious effort of personal and professional study. But it does sound as though we have started the process, according to Seth. He says, "More and more, you are beginning to deal with probabilities as you try to ascertain which of a number of probable events might physically occur. When the question of probabilities is a practical one, then scientists will give it more consideration."[28]

I'll end this chapter with this quote of Seth's, because it speaks to us of fresh beginnings and changes in the wind—just what the doctor ordered for our reality and our life. He says, "...There are points...where probabilities meet; intersections with space and time that occur in your minds while you change directions, where new probabilities that once lay latent suddenly emerge. And in terms of your civilization and your time, such a time is now."[29]

8

Consciousness is, among other things, a spontaneous exercise in creativity. You are learning now, in a three-dimensional context, the ways in which your emotional and psychic existence can create varieties of physical form. You manipulate within the psychic environment, and these manipulations are then automatically impressed upon the physical mold.
—*Seth*, Seth Speaks, *Session 515*

The Wizards of Consciousness

The majesty of the Black Elk filled his windshield, its grace of movement impressed on his mind's eye in a split second. A sight to behold, thought Andy Hauck, former member of Jane Roberts's ESP class. But in the next second it was obvious that disaster was about to occur. The elk had positioned itself directly in front of Andy's speeding car at a point in time when there was no logical action Andy could take to maneuver out of its way.

But Andy could, and did, take "illogical" action, and that action saved the life of the elk, and possibly his own as well. Without time for conscious thought, Andy nevertheless made the decision to immediately change probabilities. There was no way he was ready to accept the killing of the magnificent animal framed by his windshield, and that strong desire not to harm the elk, intertwined with Andy's knowledge of and background in probabilities, allowed time to readjust itself. The impossible occurred: The elk gracefully, and it is assumed with gratitude, repositioned itself a couple seconds ahead of where it "should" have been in the scene, and Andy's fender just missed its hind quarters by a hair's breadth.

When Katharine Newcomb was driving across country from Mississippi to Eugene, Oregon, to become gainfully employed by Seth Network International as editor of our magazine *Reality Change: The Global Seth Journal*, she hit a bad strip of road littered with thousands of tiny rocks. She found herself behind an 18-wheeler that was spewing the overgrown pebbles onto her car at a frightening velocity. To her dismay, Kat noticed several chips of glass missing from her dusty windshield. She plodded on as the grime thickened, searching for a gas station where she could check the extent of the bad news.

Along the way, and out of mild desperation, Kat decided she'd consciously play with probabilities and see if she could conjure up one free of chips in her windshield. She did just that. Through focused thought and visualization, Katharine entered a probability where not one chip remained on the windshield an hour later when the gas station attendant cleared away the dirt.

Wizards at Work

Are Andy and Katharine wizards of the highest order, or were they exerting common, everyday control over their lives? It's true that both understand probabilities to some extent and therefore have conscious tools at their fingertips, but it's also true that what they accomplished is nothing more than what all of us do, knowingly or unknowingly, when we decide to make an alteration of any magnitude in our lives: We change probabilities.

But life is not just about selecting probabilities, although that is precisely what happens with each thought we think. Life is about purpose and meaning, about learning and growing. It's about allowing ourselves the openness of mind to expand with new ideas, to see new "facts," to experience out-of-the-ordinary events without fear—indeed, with excitement. Life is about living in physical reality within a continuous psychological fullness.

I guess I felt my life was lacking such fullness in 1991, or I would not have created the situation I'm about to relate to you. It was just days before Christmas and Stan Ulkowski and I had moved into a new house in Eugene. Our neighbors came over and introduced themselves and invited us to a large party at their home the next night.

The first snow of the season fell the day of the party, and Stan and I walked next door amidst a Currier and Ives scene of winter beauty. We entered the house to warm welcomes and jovial comments. *How wonderful*, I thought, *this is a perfect pre-Christmas setting. Good will and cheer in lovely surroundings.*

At the suggestion of our host, we made our way to a huge room where at least 50 people were gathered to sing Christmas carols. We found a comfortable spot and a song book, and settled in to enjoy the evening. After the first carol or two, about the time we were singing "Silent Night," I drew my eyes away from the songbook and people, and started perusing the room. Hanging from the walls were the heads of various species of dead animals, and mounted next to the carnage were our host's war mementos—rifles and helmets and ammunition displays. Sleep in heavenly peace, we sang. I wondered if the words were meant to include the animals and the war dead.

I became exceedingly sad, almost to the point of tears.

Stan and I excused ourselves and went home. I sat alone for hours thinking of the dichotomy between the original, undistorted meaning of Christmas and the way most of us live our lives. To me the real sadness was that we never see the contradiction, so we never seek alternatives. The personal good news that arose from the evening was that I decided I could not, would not accept the contradictions any longer in my own life. I would do whatever it took to understand how to create my reality to one that is worthy of my role as eternal consciousness in physical form.

I'm not there yet, but I've made progress. So have many others, as you will read here. Some of the following stories push the boundaries of conventional thought and acceptance ...some of them are light years beyond such boundaries. Then there are the ones that seem almost ordinary in nature, simply consciousness quietly teaching itself about creation. As a composite the stories start to outline the kind of thinking that is spreading across our planet, and the types of events individuals are bringing into their private space continuums in order to learn more about this reality. People everywhere are questioning and probing, no longer willing to accept ideas they had no say in establishing as the current world view. They want a new world view, for themselves, their families and for all people who are not satisfied with the norm.

My personal stories are longer than the others, since I'm intimately familiar with the details of the events. I hope you'll enjoy these snippets of experience from consciousness seeking to understand itself.

Creation on the Fly

Over the New Year holiday between 1995 and 1996, Stan and I rented a house on the Oregon coast with Kat Newcomb and Andy Maleta. We arrived first and immediately started emptying the car of its supplies. Stan took the first load into the kitchen, and while there, studied the stove's four burners. He was the designated cook for the trip, and part of the cooking paraphernalia he had packed included an oversized pan. *Would it fit on the small stove?* he wondered. Quite nicely, it seemed. With that concern put to rest, he proceeded back to the car for his next load.

I passed him in the living room as I headed into the kitchen. Being a tea drinker, the unusual copper teapot on the stove's back burner caught my attention immediately. *How lovely,* I thought, *and quite a special treat to find in a rental home.* A few minutes later Stan joined me as I unpacked boxes on the kitchen counter. I pointed to the teapot and commented on its uniqueness. Stan asked me where I had found it, and I told him it had been sitting on the stove when I walked in. He was quiet for a moment, and then proceeded to tell me of his stove survey during his first trip into the house less than five minutes before. Clearly, he said, there had been no teapot on the burner at that time.

Wishes Becoming Objects

I met a woman in Denver who told the story of desiring a lid for a pot she had purchased that day. Later in the afternoon she walked out to her car, and there on its trunk was a pot lid that exactly fit her pan. Perhaps this Seth quote was meant for her: "It is only by comprehending the nature of this constant translation of thoughts and desires—not into words now, but into physical objects—that you can realize your true independence from circumstance, time, and environment."[1]

Communicating Via Thought

One day Stan had a message on his answer machine from a shipping agent, a man he had briefly talked to for the first time the previous day. The message was that there had been a death in the man's family and he would return Stan's call as soon as possible. Stan later filled me in on the details of the phone call, including the fact that the shipping agent's father had died. Two days later Stan received another phone call from the man. He told Stan his father had passed on, and he hadn't mentioned it in the previous message for personal reasons. As the agent made that comment, it clicked with Stan that, indeed, the man had not said in his recorded message which family member had died.

A Cold Is Not

Over New Year's I developed a humdinger of a cold. It's exceedingly uncommon for me to get sick, and if I do it's rarely with the strength with which this cold struck. I knew the reasons for the illness, but I didn't seem to have the focus to eliminate it consciously. So, I rode it out.

Then, about three months later I awoke in the middle of the night to a very scratchy throat. Oh, no! This simply could not be! I clearly remembered the weeks of illness in January, and my throat felt as sore as at the beginning of that siege. I lay in bed hating the whole thing, feeling depressed and somewhat beaten. I hadn't been able to undo the New Year's cold, I thought, so what was the probability I could do it this time? With that kind of thinking, probably zero, I decided.

So I changed my mind and gave it a go. First, I simply refused to entertain the idea that I was to be sick. I said to myself my old familiar phrase, "This is not an option." Then I decided to use the sleep state to handle the healing. As I was falling back to sleep, I asked for assistance with changing my body state to one of health. I imagined myself a few days previously, when I had been without illness. I saw how strong I looked and felt. I held the thought for awhile, and then drifted off.

The next morning I awoke to a mild case of laryngitis, a stuffy head and the sneezes, but no sore throat. Later I did a couple of visualizations and took a nap, requesting the same sort of assistance as the night before. I was somewhat weak and drained that day, but I could tell the cold was not fully operative yet. That night I again asked for help in the dream state. This time when I woke up in the middle of the night, I knew for certain that my body was being psychically healed. I felt it, and I remembered the deep activity that had been obvious in my dreams and upon surfacing into physical reality. I was quite relieved.

The next day I did another visualization and one final call for dream help that night. And then it was over. All of the symptoms had disappeared by morning's light. Nothing remained to remind me of any illness.

It's Good to See You

Joel Heath was blind in one eye and going blind in the other. The doctors said his condition was irreversible and no surgery or drugs would help. Joel, knowing that illness is caused by the mind, decided to find the beliefs that were underlying his problem. He did just that, and released them. Within 24 hours his sight started returning, and within ten days he had his vision back.

Seth says, "You can change the picture of your life at any time if only you realize that it is simply the one portrait of yourself that you have created from an unlimited amount of probable ones...If you understand the nature of probabilities, you will not need to <u>pretend</u> to ignore your present situation. You will recognize it instead as a probable reality that you have physically materialized. Taking that for granted, you will then begin the process necessary to bring a different probability into physical experience."[2]

Playing With Nature

Frank Kollins had driven the same route to his office several times a week for 15 years, enjoying the scenery. But one day the scenery changed. He passed a field where a grove of trees had grown for as long as he could remember—but they weren't there. Nothing was there except a bare field overgrown with weeds.

Who changed the scene? Seth says, "There is a physical give-and-take between the body and environment beyond that which you recognize; an inner dynamics here that escapes you...You form your environment and you are a part of it."[3]

Choices in the Now

The words, *You can make this as difficult as you want it to be*, kept running through my head. I'd been thinking a lot about how negative thoughts of the moment can color an event instantly, pulling in all sorts of little irritations when perhaps they weren't warranted, or not originally scheduled as part of the story line in Framework 2. I was running on the sand of the Oregon coast early one overcast morning, renewing my past alignment with this form of exercise.

But that morning on the beach I suspected that I wasn't making my re-entry into running as easy as it could be. I was monitoring my muscles and energy level keenly, waiting for the first sign of fatigue. I was focusing on the tightness in my calves and the crick in my knees. I was aware of each breath I took, wondering how long I could run before I'd need to stop and walk a short distance to reset it.

You can make this as difficult as you want it to be, I reminded myself. How much were my negative thoughts impacting my running, I wondered? How about significantly? *You can make this as difficult as you want it to be.* So I released my scrutiny and settled in to a slow pace as I watched the shore birds hunt for crabs as the waves receded from the sand.

Eventually ahead of me I saw a small stream that cut through the sand perpendicular to the ocean, formed by the week's rain runoff from the cliffs. From a distance it looked like a small river which would need to be forded if I were to continue running in that direction. Since I spend a good amount of time on the Oregon beaches, this phenomenon was commonplace to me. At times when I'd reach such a stream, it would be impassable; at other times, I could carefully pick my way across to the other side. As I approached the present flowing water, I thought to myself, *You can make this as difficult as you want it to be.* It "turned out" to be relatively easy to skip from high point to high point of sand with little of the deeper rushing water entering my shoes.

When I returned to the house that I was occupying for four days in the seaside town of Yachats after a longer than expected—and more pleasant than expected—run, I was chagrined to realize I'd locked myself out. *You can make this as difficult as you want it to be,* I thought, as I took stock of the situation. Since I don't lock my car and usually leave my keys inside it, I had access to a cell phone and transportation. After calling my niece Melissa and her husband Rocky, the owners of the house, and learning there was no hidden key on the premises, I drove into town and phoned a locksmith. He just happened to be on his way to work in a town further up the highway and would be driving through Yachats in a short period of time. I returned to the house, sat on some boulders writing notes, and waited, enjoying myself.

I'm convinced that each situation had potential downsides that could have been activated through more static than I was willing to allot to them. Probabilities abounded that could have driven me nuts if I'd dwelled on what the future might bring, instead of holding my intent for "ease" in the now. We meet all sorts of situations in life that have the potential to make our lives temporarily miserable; but the choice is always ours as to the attitude we will hold moment by moment. And that chosen attitude can be the telling difference between comfort and discomfort...literally. As Seth explains, "Basically, events are not built one <u>upon</u> the other. They grow <u>out of</u> each other in a kind of spontaneous expansion, a profusion of creativity, while the conscious mind chooses which aspects to experience—and those aspects then become what you call an objective event."[4]

The Power of Assumption

Nancy Walker's mother raised her and her two sisters alone, and under the circumstances, finances were tight. But going on to college was not a problem for Nancy—she had unwaveringly *assumed* from early childhood that she would attend a university...it was just something that would occur. So when she won a scholarship to the University of Northern Colorado, the news seemed anticlimactic, something to be taken in stride as a natural outgrowth of her childhood desire.

Rings of Telepathy

My daughter Cathleen and I have always exhibited a psychic closeness—we communicate on levels other than ordinary at times. When we lived in Southern California, I bought myself a lovely ring with several semiprecious stones on it. Months went by, and for reasons not remembered my daughter never saw it. Then her birthday rolled around, and on her wish list was a ring. She was at that age when it seemed prudent to let her pick her own style, so I gave her my credit card and told her to have a good time shopping for her present. After several days of looking in stores up and down the coast, she returned home with her treasure. It was an exact replica of my ring.

Heredity Unmasked

Katharine Newcomb had had a strong allergic reaction to milk products since childhood, part of a genetically transmitted hereditary pattern called lactose intolerance. And there was plenty of evidence of it in her life, including a medicine chest full of expensive lactose enzyme replacement that she'd consumed with almost every meal for several years. But one day in 1996 when she found herself presented with a celebratory meal full of milk products, she deliberately steered herself into a different probability with the thought, "What if lactose intolerance is simply a belief?" She then consumed the meal without the taking the enzyme replacement, and neither then nor since has she experienced any further reaction to dairy foods.

Seth says, "You affect the structure of your body through your thoughts. If you believe in heredity, heredity itself becomes a strong suggestive factor in your life, and can help bring about the precise malady in the body that you believed was there all along, until finally your scientific instruments uncover the 'faulty' mechanism, or whatever, and there is the evidence for all to see."[5] Perhaps Kat took to heart another quote of Seth's, though: "The point of power is in the present. Whenever possible, minimize the importance of a problem. Forget a problem and it will go away."[6]

Reports From Beyond

Sheri LoBello, Seth Network International's office manager, handed me a report one afternoon for my immediate perusal. I was rushing to get a job out, and set the report down...somewhere. Sheri soon cornered me, asking about the report's status. After a frantic search of the outer offices, she and I scanned the area by my computer; but no report. We turned away for a moment to discuss the situation, and then turned back to my computer. Our eyes caught sight of the missing report simultaneously—there it sat, snuggled up to my computer as though it had been there awhile.

Defogging Reality

Around 10:00 at night and thirty minutes from the Hartford, Connecticut, airport, the pilot activated the intercom. "Folks, the Hartford airport is socked in with fog, and it looks like we'll have to divert either to Boston or Providence. We'll keep you posted." Five minutes later: "Sorry folks, it looks dismal at this point. Our chance of landing in Hartford is very slim."

About that time Sheri LoBello came to Stan's and my seats, lowered herself next to my armrest, and we took stock of the situation. The three of us were headed to New Haven for one of SNI's largest conferences of the year, and we needed to arrive that night in order to start preparations first thing in the morning. It seemed imperative that we resolve this situation to our benefit. So it was decided that Sheri and I would visualize landing in Hartford, and Stan would encourage us onward by continuing to read his computer magazine. Sheri went back to her seat, and the visualizations started. According to timekeeper Stan, it was about four minutes later that the pilot once again activated the intercom: "Well, folks, there has been a dramatic improvement in the weather at Hartford. We will be landing shortly."

First You See Him...

But the fun didn't stop there. After we landed and were waiting at the baggage carousel for our luggage to arrive, Sheri and I resumed a conversation with a nice young man we had met before boarding the airplane in Chicago. Stan was standing next to me; the four of us were detached from the crowd, with no one behind us. I turned from Sheri and Mike for a few seconds to respond to a question Stan asked me; Sheri moved her eyes off Mike to look at me—and Mike literally disappeared into thin air. When we all turned to look at him after just seconds had passed, he simply was not there. He was nowhere in the baggage claim area, in fact. I know, because I scoured the place while we waited for the arrival of our luggage.

House Hunting of the Future

Mary Barton, author of *Soul Sight*, has logged hundreds of out-of-body experiences over the years. Before she was hired as SNI's product manager in Eugene, she lived in New Mexico with no conscious idea that she would be moving to the Northwest soon. However, another level of her consciousness knew it was a strong probability because when Mary and her husband Bob came to Eugene to search for a new home, Mary found she had already visited the one they eventually chose—in an out-of-body state months before the decision was made to move.

Another Disappearing Act

Norman Friedman, author of *Bridging Science and Spirit* and *The Hidden Domain*, had arrived at the Seth Network International offices earlier that day. Now he was following me in his rental car as I drove across town. At the upcoming corner was a school bus with a pick-up truck behind it, both stopped in the right turning lane while the bus waited for pedestrians to clear the crosswalk. I glanced in my rearview mirror to see if Norm was still behind me, and then proceeded through the intersection. As I cleared the intersection on the far side, I immediately looked in my mirror again. Norm was right behind me and the pedestrians were still in the crosswalk—but the bus and truck had disappeared.

When does creation happen? Our space-time guru says, "The moment as you think of it, then, is the creative framework through which you, the nonphysical self, constantly form corporeal reality; and through that window into earthly existence you form both its future and its past."[7]

Grouse and Ye Shall Receive

I drove to San Diego from Los Angeles and checked into a hotel. Stan was due to land at San Diego International Airport in two hours, so I decided I'd go to the downtown mall and kill time until he arrived by purchasing a replacement for a silk blouse I'd destroyed with drops of hair spray. That took all of 15 minutes. With nothing else to occupy my mind, I called United Airlines and learned Stan's plane had been delayed an hour. Oh, great. I'd left my briefcase stuffed with work sitting on the desk in the hotel room. Now what was I going to do? I walked for an hour, then went to my rental car, put the seat back and thought I'd take a nap. Instead I internally groused over not having brought something with me to fill the time void. Finally I put the car in gear and headed to the airport. Later, as Stan was putting his suitcase into the trunk of the car, I saw him lean down and move an object out of his way. I glanced over his shoulder—and there was my briefcase, all alone in the trunk.

Coincidences in Time

Bob Griggs tells the story of an acquaintance of his who, 50 years previously, had lost one of his dearest possessions—a book. Then one day the acquaintance found a copy of the book in a used bookstore thousands of miles from where he had lived when the original one was lost, and he purchased it. Months later when Bob's friend opened the book for the first time, he found his own signature on the inside cover: It was the same book the man had lost five decades before.

Seth says, "...Man forms physical objects as unselfconsciously and as automatically as he forms his own breath."8 That information does put a new spin on what we think of as "found" objects, does it not? Perhaps we should label them "rematerialized" instead.

Transitions of Reality

Stan and I have owned a house on an island in the Columbia River since 1990. In 1996 I was leaving the island via the same road we'd driven for years. Off to the right about two miles from our property I noticed an old, decrepit house I'd never seen previously on that sparsely populated piece of road. Odd, I thought. So days later when Stan arrived home from a business trip, I asked him to drive the same road and tell me if he could spot the never-before-seen house without my describing it. He came back minutes later and told me which one it was—because he had never seen it, either.

Impossible? Not according to Seth: "...You may open the door on any given day to a probable world from your immediate standpoint, and never know the difference. This happens all the time, and I mean all the time. You move through probabilities without knowing it. The transitions are literally invisible to you..."9 Well, sometimes.

Psychically Healing Animals

Cats are drawn to our house like fur to carpet. They come as adults, as kittens, as juniors. They check us out, seem to like what they see, and so many of them stick around. At times we've had upwards of 30 cats show up at feeding time, and not one of them was consciously solicited by us in any way. Some were born to mothers too skittish to take to the veterinarian's to be spayed, and others made their way to our home of their own accord, and we assume for their own reasons. The sick or needy ones get brought inside, when and if they agree to let us pick them up, and the others tuck themselves into our garage or other places on our property.

Our many cats have taught us more than all the text-books on consciousness combined. Because we love them unconditionally, Stan and I have been free to see them, and treat them, with a simple regard uncolored by other emotions. That simple regard leads us to reach out to them with whatever support is ours to offer. And that support includes psychic healing.

Not all of our cats seem to want hands-on affection. They are content to watch from afar, follow us around, come within yards, perhaps, of our outstretched hands, but then decide against any closer contact. So we name them, talk to them, feed them, make them comfortable with our presence, and love them. But once in a while one of our "wild" cats needs more from us, and the only way to assist it is through thought.

Cheddar was like that. He was about four months old when Stan and I found him lying on the deck with a badly mangled leg. As we cautiously approached, he struggled to his three healthy legs and hobbled away. The injured leg looked to our untrained eyes as though it would need amputation, and our hearts went out to Cheddar and the pain he must be feeling. I couldn't stand not doing something for him, so I decided to try psychic healing. I knew enough about consciousness to know that if Cheddar didn't want to be healed, my assistance would not help in the slightest. But if he did, well then we were in another ball game. The choice was to be his; the offer mine.

For the first two days I visualized sending Cheddar healing energy. (I remembered that Jane Roberts had done that for a woman across the country, and Seth had commented that the beam of energy Jane imagined was as real and solid as a steel beam.) Once I saw Cheddar as a part of the energy I sent his way, I visualized him standing stationary, with his "healthy" Framework 2 pattern superimposed over his damaged Framework 1 body. I saw Cheddar's mangled leg pulled up close to his body, and the pattern for a healthy leg extending from his hip. Then I asked Cheddar to start slowly lowering his sore leg into the pattern, and to stop if the procedure was too painful. The first visualization showed Cheddar extending his leg a little bit into the pattern before he chose to stop. In the next session he went a little further, letting his leg drop more into the healthy position.

Meanwhile in Framework 1 I didn't see Cheddar for two days. Then he came to eat. His leg still looked awful, but it was not held as tightly to his body for protection. I continued the visualizations for another three days, keeping my eye on Cheddar whenever he showed up at the house. His badly torn leg continued to inch itself toward the ground as the days wore on, slowly—very slowly—filling the pattern in my visualization.

Cheddar disappeared for well over a week. I feared the worst, but did a couple more visualizations before I stopped them. Then one day Stan called me to the door. There came Cheddar toward us, limping but walking on all four legs.

Time in Flux

During a conference Stan and I were moderating, a woman told us of a letter she mailed on a Friday, only to learn later, with proof to back it up, that the letter had been delivered on Thursday—the day before she mailed it.

Do you remember this quote of Seth's from the last chapter? "...There is no <u>rigid</u> placement of events. That placement is acquired. The uncoordinated child's senses, for example, may hear words that will be spoken <u>tomorrow</u>, while seeing the person who will speak them today."

Changing the Consensus Rules

Mary Rouen and her eighteen-year-old son left their home in Minneapolis, Minnesota, and headed to their neighborhood McDonald's for fast food. They had been visiting this same McDonald's for many years—so why wasn't it on the corner where it had forever been? Why was there nothing on the corner except a vacant field where no building had ever stood—or so it seemed from outward appearances?

Where indeed. The answer lies in Mary's and her son's agreement on which probabilities they would select and insert into physical reality. Obviously, they chose to be avant-garde and ignore the telepathic messages of the masses that said, yes, please do create your version of McDonald's on that corner so we can all play the game together. But Mary and her son changed the rules, because they had a right to do so in their space continuums.

Cosmic Assistance

Daisy, one of the more skittish of our cats, fell 15 feet onto a wood stove and broke her shoulder one day, and because she was immobile, Stan was able to pick her up and rush her to the vet's—one of the few times either of us had had our hands on her. When her hospital stay ended, I went to pick her up. Out comes the technician carrying Daisy in her arms instead of the cat carrier I had provided. *Oh no*, I thought, *this could be trouble.*

About then Daisy flung herself out of the technician's arms and ran out an open door into the pouring rain. My heart thudding, I tore after her. The poor baby was scared silly, and so was I. She ran back and forth under the same four cars, frantic with fright. My main concern was that she'd head into a huge open field leading to a residential neighborhood, and I'd never see her again. I got on my knees and pleaded with her to come to me. Fat chance, seeing that she'd never done it before under quiet, serene conditions at home, let alone in this wet, chaotic environment with traffic rushing by on the busy thoroughfare.

Finally, out of desperation, I forced myself to be calm and asked my inner self to help me. *Please, please send Daisy to me. I really need your help with this.* Not a minute later Daisy rushed out from under the car where I knelt right into my outstretched arms, and she never flinched as I walked her, cooing in her ear, across the parking lot to our car.

A couple of weeks later, Daisy had to go back to the vet's to have a pin removed from her broken shoulder, and I dreaded the approach of the day. Since we'd arrived home after the parking lot incident, Daisy had only come close enough to the house to get her food and then off she'd run with her pals.

On the pin-removal morning, I scanned the river's grass for Daisy to no avail. So, one more time I asked my inner self for assistance. *If Daisy wants me to help her, please send her to me. And, by the way, thanks in advance.* I set out Daisy's cat carrier and then went about my morning's chores. Within the hour Daisy sauntered into the house, and I casually picked her up and placed her in her carrier.

Free Will of Consciousness

Another cat story was similar, in some ways. Nutmeg, another skittish cat at the time (now we can't keep him off our laps) had a very swollen paw, and I made an appointment to take him to the veterinarian the next day. He disappeared that night, and the next morning I set his carrier out and said to my inner self, *If Nutmeg wants to go to the vet's, please tell him the time is near for departure.* Since Nutmeg has a strong dislike of the cat carrier and usually runs from its presence, I worked hard to keep the faith. But pretty soon there he was, poking his nose into the open container. All I had to do was give his bottom a light push, and in he went.

Now, Cinnamon is just the opposite of Daisy and Nutmeg. From the time he was two months old and came to us half starved, he barely leaves our sight. But on the day of his scheduled vet's visit for a sore paw, he disappeared first thing in the morning. I said to my inner self the same litany as with Nutmeg: *If Cinnamon wants to go to the vet's, please tell him the time is near for departure.*

Well, he never showed up. In fact, he was gone for 24 hours. When he did finally come home, he walked easier on his sore paw, and within a couple more days it was completely healed. My take is that Cinnamon simply decided he didn't need my help this time around, thank you very much.

Testing the Waters of Creativity

A talk show radio host told me she first heard of the concept of visualization on radio one day, but the how-tos were not discussed. It caught her imagination, though, so when she and her husband were driving Manhattan frantically searching for a parking place near the Empire State Building—a task proving to be prodigious on a beautiful weekend day—she decided to give visualization a try. While her skeptical husband drove, she started seeing a parking place near their destination. Within minutes a spot was vacated less than two blocks from the Empire State Building.

That little exercise excited her, so she gave it another try in a different way. She and her husband were headed to a Broadway play when she realized she had forgotten to pack her comb. Almost in panic, she started visualizing one coming in to her reality. As she stepped out of their car at the curbside parking place, there lay a comb on the sidewalk at her feet. She sterilized it under hot water in the theater's bathroom, and happily combed her hair.

Bouncing In and Out

I awoke one day from a nap and found myself in another probability. Instead of windows to the left of me where they were when I fell asleep, there was a solid wall. And above my head was a row of skylights, none of which should have been there. I closed my eyes and assumed that when I opened them I'd be back in the probability I'd left prior to sleep. And I was.

The Fluid Past

A man at one of our conferences told us his wife had been treated by the same doctor for over two years. One day she returned to the doctor's suite only to find someone else in his office. It seems no one in the area had ever heard of her doctor.

Did the woman change her past? It surely seems she did. Seth says, "You may say, 'I was born in a house on a certain street in a certain town, and no present belief to the contrary will change that fact.' If, in the present, one past event can be altered within your neuronal structure, however, then basically no event is safe from such change."[10]

Bridging Realities

In 1990 Stan and I were new to the Northwest. We'd moved to Oregon from California just months before, and now had bought a second home in Washington. Since Stan was busy in Eugene, it fell upon me to drive often to Washington to arrange our household goods and prepare the house for summer, among other things.

My route from Oregon into Washington took me north on Interstate 5 across the Columbia River, the border between the states. Every time I reached the river, I had a decision to make: which of the two side-by-side bridges spanning the Columbia to take? Over a period of time I tested each of them. The one I entered from the far right lane was the older of the two, its lanes narrower, and the paving bumpier. Eventually I chose to always drive across the newer bridge, the one I entered from the far left lane. The decision was made; I never thought about it again.

I never thought about it again for six years, that is, until it hit me full force one day. I turned to Stan one morning and exclaimed, "What happened to the two bridges over the Columbia?!" He looked puzzled and said, "What two bridges?" You see, there is only one bridge that spans the Columbia River north of Portland on Interstate 5.

On the Move With Visualization

Matt and Mary Harris lived in a small town in Illinois, and longed to move to Denver. Matt was doing very well in his career and making substantial money, and he and Mary saw little practical way they could make Denver happen without taking a cut in income. But instead of despairing, they decided to visualize what they wanted. Six weeks later Matt's company opened an "unexpected" office in Denver, Matt was promoted and the family relocated.

The Rainbow of Desire

As Jane Roberts wrote, through the words of Oversoul Seven in *Oversoul Seven and the Museum of Time*, "Miracles are nature unimpeded." *Something* was unimpeded when I experienced what most of the world would call a miracle. Perhaps it was me.

I was within days of finishing this book in December, 1996, yet my schedule afforded me little time to apply the focus necessary to wrap it up. The solution: go to the Oregon coast for days and do nothing but write and walk. The day Stan and I arrived my mind was filled with the ideas you've read so far in *Wizards*. They buzzed around my bonnet with an intensity I love. I'm happier than a pig in mud when my mind stretches with ideas, and writing this book has kept Seth's incredible concepts right up front in my thinking.

So by the time my feet touched the ground at Cannon Beach, I was high on the idea of *easily* creating my experiences by becoming a conscious co-creator with my inner self. The more I had studied what Seth says about a loving and supportive inner self, the purpose and meaning behind consciousness, and the implications of simultaneous time and probabilities, the more natural it seemed to be able to join in conscious partnership with the forces that be. Not that any of this was new to me, or that I hadn't touched the feeling many times before, but for some reason it was heightened on this particular afternoon.

After we unpacked the car, I left Stan to fire up the wood stove while I walked on the beach. It was late afternoon, and only four or five people were strewn along the miles of sand. Storm clouds hung over the area, yet the horizon was clear of them. The vivid winter sun, a fireball of color, had partially sunk into the water, creating a peach-colored sky far out over the Pacific. The dark clouds up close, the orange tinted horizon and the sun on fire combined to create the kind of magnificent beauty that speaks to the souls of Man.

I walked. I thought. I felt so comfortable.

About ten minutes into my walk I laughed out loud and told my inner self I'd really like to see a rainbow. Yes, a rainbow would be perfect for the scene and mood. Yes, I'd really like to see one, please.

Then I took stock of my surroundings, and wondered briefly about the plausibility of a rainbow being created at dusk, with only a sliver of sun left on the horizon. Some dim memory of the physics behind a rainbow suggested my request might be difficult for the universe to fill. After all, did not a rainbow require light to interact with water droplets?

Well, that was not my problem, I decided. Mine was to ask for what I wanted and expect it to occur. So I kept walking and asking and occasionally swiveling my head to search for my rainbow. The last of the sun disappeared into the horizon. I kept walking and asking and occasionally swiveling my head to search for my rainbow.

Then the miracle began.

I glanced at the horizon, and a rim of sun shone where none had been moments before. Interesting, I thought, as I kept walking and asking and swiveling. Then I glanced again to the west, and there was more than a sliver of sun on the horizon. I stopped walking and asking and stared at the far edge of the ocean. Over a period of perhaps a minute the sun rose to half its size. As I turned to look in the direction of our rented house, I saw it...my rainbow hung above a hill next to the house. I burst into tears.

I cried with the joy of it all, the pure, unmitigated joy of knowing my intimate connection with nature, with my inner self, with life. I cried for the ease of creation when nothing stands in the way, when harmony is reached between the conscious self and the inner self, when nature flows unimpeded. And then I watched as the sun dipped back below the horizon, and the rain started and my rainbow disappeared. I have never felt so at ease in physical reality as I did on that wet walk back to Stan.

> "You are biologically connected, chemically connected with the Earth that you know; but since it is also formed naturally and spontaneously from your own projected psychic energy, since you and the seasons even have a psychic interaction, then the self must be understood in a far greater context."[11]

9

In the next century, the inner nature of man...will free itself from many constraints that have bound it. A new era will indeed begin—not, now, a heaven on earth, but a far more sane and just world, in which man is far more aware of his relationship with his planet and of his freedom within time.

—*Seth*, Seth Speaks, *Session 586*

High Stepping Into the Future

The magnificent saga of consciousness experiencing physical life continues. From history spew stories of greatness and beauty, of violence and hatred. The intricate loveliness of certain time periods holds us in awe, while the baseness of others appalls us. Earth-tuned consciousness holds court through the ages, learning lessons and partaking of the fruits of experience offered in the medium of physical reality. Through it all scholars and philosophers have tried to make sense of the flowing drama, to chart the growth and expansion of human understanding based on a historical perspective, viewing each century as an outgrowth of the previous one. They look to the past to determine the development of the species.

But consciousness doesn't predicate its next world drama

on the past; it selects it from the inner ones churning within the minds and souls of the personalities inhabiting the globe in the present. That's the way it's been since the beginning of time; the inner becomes the outer. Take the birth of religions, for example. Ever unfolding spiritual values develop within earth's human population as its mass comprehensions move in new directions. As the deep need to experience these comprehensions in concrete terms reaches a certain intensity and mass, the framework for a new religion is established in the field of probabilities. Eventually certain consciousnesses will agree to enter physical life to act out the crucial roles needed to launch the religious drama, and once ensconced on earth ...well, let the play begin.

As long as the developing religion accurately expresses the inner experience of the consciousnesses which formed it or the later consciousnesses which will sustain it, that religion will remain a structure in physical reality. But if it tries to redesign the outer representation of the inner framework through dogma, laws and distorted symbols that have nothing to do with the interior validity from which it sprang, the religion will fade from the scene. The fading may be a quiet mass withdrawal from a church by its members, or it may be tie-breakings fraught with upheaval or killing. But once the church no longer reflects what its followers intuitively know is a true representation of their spiritual reality, they will withdraw their energy, one way or another. For as Seth says, "At no time will any church find itself in a position in which it can effectively curtail the inner experience of its members—it will only seem to do so. The forbidden experiences will simply be unconsciously expressed, gather strength and vitality, and rise up to form a counter projection which will then form another, newer exterior religious drama."[1] Of course, Seth's quote can be applied to any structure which has been thought into existence by consciousness reflecting its inner reality, from governments to societies. He says, "The structure of the psyche of the world at any given time can be ascertained by viewing its exterior condition: the various civilizations all representing actualized characteristics inherent in the world mind."[2] When the structures we've created become too distorted, they will begin to wobble. It may take time, in our terms, but once the consciousnesses involved finish sorting out what they do and do not want out of life, and what they know will bring them the most value fulfillment, they will take action to bring about the desired results.

Is there an all-powerful thought that can set fire to the world's imagination and launch substantial change? What newly held assumption will free our minds enough to create a world without fear and aggression and horror and desperation—and instead create a world laced with global camaraderie, health and fulfillment for all? Here's a clue in a quote from Seth: "I have told you often that you do yourselves a grave injustice by limiting your conception of the self. Your sense of identity, freedom, power, and love would be immeasurably enhanced if you could understand that what you are does not end at the boundaries of your skin, but continues outward through the physical environment that seems to be impersonal, or not-self."[3]

We will never understand or change our world by simply observing the physical manifestations of our idea constructions. They tell us a story that is only partially complete, but we've come to believe it's the whole picture. We accept it with all its distortions and limitations. We need another frame of reference in order to massively expand our understanding and light the freedom fires of the psyche, a point somewhere outside our own physical system which will help broaden our outlook. Such a point can only focus on the inner self since it is the seat of our multidimensionality...the seat of our creativity...the seat of our creations.

Getting back in touch with our multidimensionality and, therefore, our inner self is of paramount importance to the formation of a world at peace with itself. Through our acceptance of one time line, one world, one universe, a personified God and an individual's supposed powerlessness, we've come to believe the problems of the world are based on our lack of "spirituality." We think we're out of synch with the godly part of the universe—why else would there be such pain on earth? Draped in New Age vestments, and perhaps called Higher Self instead of God, we seek resolutions to our problems from this holier-than-us symbology. So off we go one more time, charging toward a solution that is not a solution. For as Seth says, "You will not find yourself by running from teacher to teacher, from book to book. You will not meet yourself through following any particular specialized method of meditation. Only by looking quietly within the self that you know can your own reality be experienced..."[4]

We are right now and ever more spiritual beings. Our spirituality is not in question or in need of sprucing up. If we move our focus off spirituality per se and instead look at physical reality from a different slant, one focused on sensing the multidimensionality and creative aspects of consciousness, everything shifts into perspective. No longer do we misunderstand the genesis of physical reality, so we no longer seek absolution from outside ourselves. The buck starts and stops with our creative consciousnesses, the same place our spirituality resides. As one mystic mentor says, "True spirituality is a thing of joy and of the earth, and has nothing to do with fake adult dignity. It has nothing to do with long words and sorrowful faces. It has to do with the dance of consciousness that is within you, and with the sense of spiritual adventure that is within your hearts."[5]

Touchstone Knowledge

So, what happened? If we are spiritual beings, literal parts of All That Is, how did that knowledge ever escape us? And how did we come to create a world seemingly quite at odds with our heritage? Here's a little history lesson that may shed light on how we got to where we are today and how we can get out of it tomorrow.

Seth says, "Using your free will, you have made physical reality something quite different than what was intended. You have allowed the ego to become overly developed and overly specialized...You were to work out problems and challenges, but you were always to be aware of your own inner reality, and of your nonphysical existence. To a large extent you have lost contact with this."[6] Our race made choices eons ago to develop our belief in an exterior environment apart from ourselves, one we supposedly had no hand in creating or impacting. We did well in developing the belief, and as it grew we started to forget our true oneness with all things, and instead started to see separation of all things. We placed God outside ourselves, nature outside ourselves, and we created a world without obvious, acknowledged meaning and purpose. But what had to happen to our belief system in order to bring about such a strong assumption of separation in the first place? It's rather simple, really. We had to hold the primary belief that the intellect is our sole source of information. That's all it took.

Why? Why would that one belief cause such hardships globally and personally? It has to do with the fact that feelings, thoughts, attitudes and beliefs create private and world reality—and fear is an intense feeling. Seth says, "The intellect, then, <u>can</u> and does form strong paranoid tendencies when it is put in the position of believing that it must solve all personal problems alone."[7] He says the intellect senses a deep powerlessness when this occurs, for to an extent it is philosophically cut off from its own source of energy and power.

Paranoid tendencies form when we feel vulnerable to events over which we think we have no control. When we fear for our health, our wealth, our families, our very lives, we become paranoid. We might never tag the low-level feeling of anxiety that colors our decisions and forms our choices as paranoia. Indeed, we'd probably feel we were rationally solving daily and long-term life issues by cautiously scanning the downside for potential problems and taking appropriate protective measures.

But what leads to that rational caution, according to Seth, is a feeling that we're on our own here, stand-alone matter formed by chance, with the need to protect ourselves from harm by our wits alone. And so we, in essence, become fearful. And since we create our reality through our thoughts, attitudes and beliefs, our reality starts to mirror back to us *why* we should be fearful. We see crime at every turn, from petty infractions in the office to murder on our streets; we see our body start to break down before our very eyes, the victim of time, accidents and diseases; and we experience competition and survival of the fittest in the workplace and the world place.

This is all just too much to bear without taking serious action! Protection is the answer...isn't it? There seems to be no other means of controlling our existence, except through protective measures. So on the global front we build bigger weapons, develop more medicines, create stronger prisons, launch more wars. And on the private front we purchase more weapons, take more medicines, pay for stronger prisons, and fight more wars—all in the name of protection.

But we're taking the wrong actions. We're fighting the *results* of our fears, instead of addressing the *cause* of our fears. And, according to Seth, the basic underlying cause of our fear is our belief that there is no assistance and support from an inner world, that the intellect is all that is. He says that when we follow the so-called rational approach to life, the approach that suggests nothing is of value unless it comes from the exterior world of facts and figures, we cannot help but feel threatened and separated, with a division between the spiritual and physical, because the rational approach goes against what he calls "life's directives and life's natural rhythms."

The solution to long-term resolution of private and global problems is simple, then. We redefine the role of the intellect and start using the magical approach to life, the approach that takes it for granted that we are cradled by a greater reality that sustains us with comfort and security and answers. Seth starts us on our way with this quote from *The Magical Approach*: "First of all, if you realize that the intellect itself <u>is a part of</u> nature, a part of the natural person, a part of magical processes, then you need not overstrain it, force it to feel isolated, or put it in a position in which paranoid tendencies develop. It is itself supported, as your intuitions are, by life's magical processes. It is supported by the greater energy that gave you and the world birth."[8]

The intellect is meant to work hand in hand with the intuitive side of our nature. Our inner self communicates with us moment by moment by using the inner senses. Some forms of its more obvious communications are through intuition, insight, impulses and dreams. By using the magical approach to life, we open our self to great amounts of information not available to the intellect alone. Just as soon as the intellect accepts that there is an inner world from which all else springs, that that inner world holds knowledge far surpassing what is seen in the outer world, and that we can sense that knowledge and apply it to our daily concerns, the fear starts to melt...and we're using the magical approach.

The magical approach to life is a blending of the intellect and our intuitive side. When the intellect starts to fear a future event because it can't determine its outcome, it can use the magical approach to alleviate its concern and help build that future event to its liking. In other words, the intellect can share the load of life with another portion of itself, a portion which is in a far better position to assess the situation and suggest new directions, if appropriate. The intellect finds that it no longer has to go it alone—and that is exceedingly good news.

Many people in today's world are starting to understand just how much homage has been paid the intellect in the past. However, at times they seem to go overboard in their criticism of it. They see the intellect as a culprit, something to be tamed into submission by the emerging intuitional portion of the psyche. In attempting to overcompensate for the role the intellect has played in creating the belief in separation, and in a misunderstanding of its purpose, the intellect has been knocked by some of the best of the New Age. But according to Seth, it's not that we overuse the intellect; it's that we rely upon it exclusively and don't naturally accept other means of gathering information and other methods of making decisions.

The intellect is not the bad guy, and intuition is not the white hat. Seth, in fact, calls the intellect brilliant. It was, after all, put in place by our inner selves as a tool for assessing current life conditions and then making decisions based on those assessments. The intellect's focus and intent is what forms our individual realities. It creates the thoughts, attitudes and beliefs that become exteriorized as events. On the larger scale, our joint intellects form the world picture in the same way. It is the intellect's expectations and beliefs that direct our experience in the world, privately and *en masse*.

And that is precisely why we must assure that the intellect does not become paranoid. Seth says, "If the intellect believes that the world is a threat to existence, then that belief will alter its intent...The beliefs of the intellect operate then as powerful suggestions...so that there is little distance between the intellect and the beliefs that it holds as true."[9] Seth is saying that we get what we "hold as true," and what we hold as true can alter the intent, or direction, of the world. As a civilization, what we hold as true today leads to aggressive protection, and that doesn't particularly bode well for a future of peace and security, and it certainly can't move us into a probability where new understandings are in place and used.

What we hold as true must change. It must encompass a knowledge of the much larger reality of which we are all a part, and it must include a belief in our inner self. We must allow our inner self to help us, but we can't do that until we believe in it. Once we do, we can then utilize the magical approach to life, the approach that is a blending of intuition and intellect—the approach that is the solution to the creation of a new civilization.

And what of those of us who believe such outlandish ideas right now, who hold them in our hearts as true? Seth has a few private words for us: "I have said to you before—using, if you will forgive me—your terms, that you are the black sheep of the universe, because you no longer blame gods nor devils nor circumstances for those effects in your life that you do not like; nor bow down to gods, devils, or circumstances in praise for those good conditions that you have yourselves created. That therefore, you will become conscious co-creators with an All That Is that has little to do with the puny concepts in which God has been entrapped for centuries, as far as your religions and myths are concerned. For those myths have also entrapped you who believed in them."[10]

The Future Agenda

There must be a bunch of black sheep in today's world, or people who will hold the title shortly. As noted earlier in this chapter, when enough individual consciousnesses have had it, when their exterior worlds no longer reflect value fulfillment, let alone happiness and excitement, they will bring about the changes necessary to redefine life. Well, hold on to the brim of your psychic hat—it seems as a group we're on our way. If probabilities are an accurate barometer of world thought, major change has a strong possibility of occurring soon.

While our race seems to have gotten itself into quite a pickle in this reality we call home, with the end of civilization as we know it prophesied by many, the cavalry is approaching at full speed. While it's true that no events are predestined, it is also true that a framework has been set in the field of probabilities by our collective inner selves which can allow our civilization to reorganize itself with new understandings paving the way. And it seems our race is close to choosing that framework. The changes which will bring about the new framework are being psychically contemplated by earth-tuned consciousness as we speak. If we decide to slip sideways into this new probability, its framework will more than likely be in place physically by 2075, and is actually in developmental stages now, according to Seth. And what do you suppose the new civilization will be based upon? The fact that—big surprise—consciousness is multidimensional, eternal, exceedingly creative, and literally all there is.

What does it take to move our world into the probability where such incredible news is commonplace knowledge? A change of mass beliefs, and that's one reason the globe has been awash in other-world input from a variety of sources in recent decades, and why Seth made his appearance in Jane's and Rob's home in 1963. In his case he says, "...Not only have I been trying to divest you of official ideas, but to prepare you for the acceptance of a new version of reality; a version that could be described in many fashions. It has been during the annals of history, but many of those fashions also indisputably, and with the best of intentions, managed to give a faulty picture: You ended up with your gods and demons, unwieldy methods and cults, and often with the intellect downgraded. I hope, of course, that our 'model' avoids many of those pitfalls."[11]

The model Seth is talking about is based on certain assumptions which will probably be accepted by the majority of earth's people. They are not laws, but ideas which will be held as true. In *Psychic Politics*, Jane lists these assumptions, called codicils for reference, after being introduced to them while in an altered state of consciousness. She says, "...I knew that the material to come represented an alternate model for civilization to follow...a model that we hadn't chosen in the past. The codicils would represent a fresh hypothesis upon which to build a new, better civilization."[12]

There are twelve codicils and many of them are complex, so I'll not list them here. However, the first codicil is worth noting, because it sets the stage, by assumption, for the emerging world: *All of creation is sacred and alive, each part connected to each other part, and each communicating in a creative cooperative commerce in which the smallest and largest are equally involved.*

What would a civilization be like that treated the first codicil as truth and integrated the idea that consciousness is multidimensional and one into the fabric of its days? Seth tells us that "No man will look down upon an individual from another race...no sex will be considered better than the other...consciousness will feel its connections with all other living beings...children will be taught that basic identity is not dependent upon the body, and that time as you know it is an illusion...many of the lessons 'that come with age' will then be available to the young...the old will not lose the spiritual elasticity of their youth...brain mappings will be possible in which past-life memories are evoked...psychic frameworks rather than physical ones (will) form the foundations for civilization."[13]

What this will translate into is unprecedented change. For instance, all governments and social structures will be altered radically, because they will be based on a belief in the sacredness, and therefore equality, of each individual. Science and psychology will be completely revamped to fit within the emerging framework's assumption that consciousness creates everything, and therefore life in general and individual creature life is imbued with great meaning and purpose. Religion will become a personal, individual experience, no longer dogmatized by large organizations. The medical profession will become the secondary framework of healing to an individual's primary interaction with his or her inner self, helping to sort out beliefs and suggest treatment based on the psychic makeup of the individual. Our learning centers will teach the joy of creativity, gently nudging us to explore and develop our conscious creation skills and consciously determined professions and lifestyles that best suit our inner purpose. And our courts of law will settle issues by using tools inherent in all consciousness, such as focusing the inner senses to track a problem back to its source (even, perhaps, in another lifetime), and offer solutions based on a much broader understanding of the individual.

And what of our personal lives? How will our intimate daily experience differ from today's? If we choose to, we will lead our lives with no unusual concerns facing us, no excessive worry, depression or desperation. Our bodies will react to our goodwill by mirroring it back to us in the form of health and well being. We will share fine moments with friends who seek the same value fulfillment we seek, leading to conversations laden with a unique psychological fullness. Our security will be assured, because we will so trust the rightness of our being. We will understand our deep connection with other species, and so treat animals as friends and companions instead of possessions and targets. The development of our psychic abilities will open rich worlds of exploration and experience. We will be active, aware participants in our dream world, reaching into the very source of our selves. In a nutshell, it will be a sane and solid world without major impediments, in which the opposites of despair and apathy reign.

Our awesome new civilization hinges on our acceptance of knowledge we have submerged for a long, long time. But we always knew our path of separation was simply an experiment in consciousness and that we would return to our roots eventually. Seth says, "Even when you lost sight—as you knew you would—of those deep connections, they would continue to operate until, in its own way, man's consciousness could rediscover the knowledge and put it to use —deliberately and willfully, thereby bringing that consciousness to flower. In your terms this would represent a great leap, for the egotistically aware individual would fully comprehend unconscious knowledge and <u>act on his own</u>, out of choice. He would become a conscious co-creator."[14]

The Greatest Endeavor of All Time

Wizards of consciousness are what we are, couched in an inviolate naturalness, with psychic roots anchored in greater dimensions. We form a brotherhood with all living things and share an inner empathy that connects us all. We are learning the skills of consciousness, the consummate lessons needed to grow beyond limits. Seth encourages us onward with these words: "Each person alive helps paint the living picture of civilization as it exists at any given time...Be your own best artist. Your thoughts, feelings and expectations are like the living brush strokes with which you paint your corner of life's landscape. If you do your best in your own life, then you are indeed helping improve the quality of all life. Your thoughts are as real as snowflakes or raindrops or clouds. They mix and merge with the thoughts of others, to form man's livingscape, providing the vast mental elements from which physical events will be formed."[15]

As consciousness, we constantly strive toward value fulfillment. When we reach it we will have created the greatest civilization ever to inhabit the face of the earth. The time has come to make it happen.

"You can become involved now in a new exploration, one in which man's civilizations and organizations change their course, reflecting his good intents and his ideals. You can do this by seeing to it that each step you personally take is 'ideally suited' to the ends you hope to achieve...If you do this, your life will automatically be provided with excitement, natural zest and creativity, and those characteristics will be reflected outward into the social, political, economic, and scientific worlds. This is a challenge more than worth the effort. It is a challenge that I hope each reader will accept. The practical idealist...When all is said and done, there is no other kind.

"I bid each of you success in that endeavor."[16]

Notes

Introduction

1. A complete listing of books by Jane Roberts and Seth is found in "Suggested Reading."

Chapter 1: *The Straight Scoop From a Dead William James*

1. The three "world view" books written by Jane Roberts are *The Afterdeath Journal of an American Philosopher: The World View of William James; The World View of Paul Cezanne;* and *The World View of Rembrandt Van Rijn. Rembrandt* has not been published to date, and *James* and *Cezanne* are temporarily out of print.

2. Jane Roberts, *The "Unknown" Reality, Volume Two* (San Rafael, Calif.: Amber-Allen Publishing, 1996), Session 718.

3. Jane Roberts, *The Afterdeath Journal of an American Philosopher* (New York: Prentice Hall Press, 1987), Chapter 10, p. 162.

4. Jane Roberts, *The Afterdeath Journal of an American Philosopher* (New York: Prentice Hall Press, 1987), Chapter 10, p. 163.

5. Jane Roberts, *The Afterdeath Journal of an American Philosopher* (New York: Prentice Hall Press, 1987), Chapter 10, p. 166.

6. Jane Roberts, *The Seth Material* (New York: Prentice

Hall Press, 1987), Chapter 18, p. 245.

7. A gestalt is defined by *Webster's New Collegiate Dictionary* as "...a structure, configuration, or pattern of physical, biological, or psychological phenomena so integrated as to constitute a functional unit with properties not derivable from its parts in summation."

8. Jane Roberts, *Seth Speaks: The Eternal Validity of the Soul* (San Rafael, Calif.: Amber-Allen/New World Library, 1994), Session 582.

9. Jane Roberts, *The Afterdeath Journal of an American Philosopher* (New York: Prentice Hall Press, 1987), Chapter 6, p. 110.

10. Jane Roberts, *Seth Speaks: The Eternal Validity of the Soul* (San Rafael, Calif.: Amber-Allen/New World Library, 1994), Session 520.

11. Jane Roberts, *The Afterdeath Journal of an American Philosopher* (New York: Prentice Hall Press, 1987), Chapter 7, p. 118.

12. Jane Roberts, *The Afterdeath Journal of an American Philosopher* (New York: Prentice Hall Press, 1987), Chapter 7, p. 120.

13. Jane Roberts, *The Afterdeath Journal of an American Philosopher* (New York: Prentice Hall Press, 1987), Chapter 12, p. 188.

14. Jane Roberts, *Seth Speaks: The Eternal Validity of the Soul* (San Rafael, Calif.: Amber-Allen/New World Library, 1994), Session 547.

Chapter 2: Am I My Own Grandma?

1. Jane Roberts, *The Nature of the Psyche: Its Human Expression* (San Rafael, Calif.: Amber-Allen Publishing, 1996), Session 787.

2. Jane Roberts, *Seth Speaks: The Eternal Validity of the Soul* (San Rafael, Calif.: Amber-Allen/New World Library,

1994), Session 512.

3. Jane Roberts, *How to Develop Your ESP Power* (Hollywood, Florida: Lifetime Books, Inc., 1993), Chapter 11, p. 191.

4. Jane Roberts, *How to Develop Your ESP Power* (Hollywood, Florida: Lifetime Books, Inc., 1993), Chapter 11, p. 191.

5. Jane Roberts, *The "Unknown" Reality, Volume Two* (San Rafael, Calif.: Amber-Allen Publishing, 1996), Session 722.

6. Jane Roberts, *Seth Speaks: The Eternal Validity of the Soul* (San Rafael, Calif.: Amber-Allen/New World Library, 1994), Session 589.

7. Jane Roberts, *Seth Speaks: The Eternal Validity of the Soul* (San Rafael, Calif.: Amber-Allen/New World Library, 1994), Appendix, p. 424.

8. Jane Roberts, *The "Unknown" Reality, Volume Two* (San Rafael, Calif.: Amber-Allen Publishing, 1996), Session 724.

9. Jane Roberts, *Seth Speaks: The Eternal Validity of the Soul* (San Rafael, Calif.: Amber-Allen/New World Library, 1994), Session 590.

10. Jane Roberts, *The "Unknown" Reality, Volume One* (San Rafael, Calif.: Amber-Allen Publishing, 1996), Session 680.

11. Jane Roberts, *The "Unknown" Reality, Volume One* (San Rafael, Calif.: Amber-Allen Publishing, 1996), Session 680.

12. Jane Roberts, *The "Unknown" Reality, Volume Two* (San Rafael, Calif.: Amber-Allen Publishing, 1996), Session 740.

13. Jane Roberts, *The "Unknown" Reality, Volume Two* (San Rafael, Calif.: Amber-Allen Publishing, 1996), Session 732.

14. Jane Roberts, *The "Unknown" Reality, Volume Two* (San Rafael, Calif.: Amber-Allen Publishing, 1996), Session

734.

15. Jane Roberts, *The "Unknown" Reality, Volume Two* (San Rafael, Calif.: Amber-Allen Publishing, 1996), Session 735.

16. Jane Roberts, *The Afterdeath Journal of an American Philosopher* (New York: Prentice Hall Press, 1987), Chapter 8, p. 138.

17. Jane Roberts, *The "Unknown" Reality, Volume One* (San Rafael, Calif.: Amber-Allen Publishing, 1996), Session 681.

18. Jane Roberts, *The Afterdeath Journal of an American Philosopher* (New York: Prentice Hall Press, 1987), Chapter 6, p. 113.

Chapter 3: Consciousness in Physical Attire

1. Jane Roberts, *The Nature of Personal Reality* (San Rafael, Calif.: Amber-Allen/New World Library, 1994), Session 615.

2. Jane Roberts, *The Seth Material* (New York: Prentice Hall Press, 1987), Chapter 13, p. 163.

3. Jane Roberts, *Seth Speaks: The Eternal Validity of the Soul* (San Rafael, Calif.: Amber-Allen/New World Library, 1994), Appendix, Session 596.

4. Jane Roberts, *The Seth Material* (New York: Prentice Hall Press, 1987), Appendix, Session 506.

5. Jane Roberts, *The Seth Material* (New York: Prentice Hall Press, 1987), Chapter 16, p. 216.

6. Jane Roberts, *The Nature of Personal Reality* (San Rafael, Calif.: Amber-Allen/New World Library, 1994), Session 615.

7. Jane Roberts, *Seth, Dreams and Projections of Consciousness* (Walpole, N.H.: Stillpoint Publishing, 1986), Chapter 12, Session 181.

8. Jane Roberts, *The Nature of Personal Reality* (San Rafael,

Calif.: Amber-Allen/New World Library, 1994), Session 615.

9. Jane Roberts, *Seth Speaks: The Eternal Validity of the Soul* (San Rafael, Calif.: Amber-Allen/New World Library, 1994), Session 546.

10. Jane Roberts, *The Individual and the Nature of Mass Events* (San Rafael, Calif.: Amber-Allen Publishing, 1995), Session 803.

11. Jane Roberts, *The Individual and the Nature of Mass Events* (San Rafael, Calif.: Amber-Allen Publishing, 1995), Session 857.

12. Jane Roberts, *The Individual and the Nature of Mass Events* (San Rafael, Calif.: Amber-Allen Publishing, 1995), Session 856.

13. Jane Roberts, *The God of Jane: A Psychic Manifesto* (Englewood Cliffs, N.J.: Prentice-Hall, Inc., 1981), Chapter 18, Session 872.

14. Jane Roberts, *Seth Speaks: The Eternal Validity of the Soul* (San Rafael, Calif.: Amber-Allen/New World Library, 1994), Session 572.

15. Jane Roberts, *The Afterdeath Journal of an American Philosopher* (New York: Prentice Hall Press, 1987), Chapter 13, p. 194.

16. Jane Roberts, *The Afterdeath Journal of an American Philosopher* (New York: Prentice Hall Press, 1987), Chapter 13, p. 194-5.

17. Jane Roberts, *How to Develop Your ESP Power* (Hollywood, Florida: Lifetime Books, Inc., 1993), Chapter 1, p. 21.

18. Jane Roberts, *The Individual and the Nature of Mass Events* (San Rafael, Calif.: Amber-Allen Publishing, 1995), Session 823.

19. Jane Roberts, *Seth Speaks: The Eternal Validity of the Soul* (San Rafael, Calif.: Amber-Allen/New World Library, 1994), Session 589.

20. Jane Roberts, *Seth, Dreams and Projections of Conscious-*

ness (Walpole, N.H.: Stillpoint Publishing, 1986), Chapter 8, p. 141.

Chapter 4: Stretching Toward Value Fulfillment

1. Jane Roberts, *The Afterdeath Journal of an American Philosopher* (New York: Prentice Hall Press, 1987), Chapter 10, p. 164.

2. Jane Roberts, *The Individual and the Nature of Mass Events* (San Rafael, Calif.: Amber-Allen Publishing, 1995), Session 801.

3. Jane Roberts, *The Nature of Personal Reality* (San Rafael, Calif.: Amber-Allen/New World Library, 1994), Session 654.

4. Jane Roberts, Introductory Essays and Notes by Robert F. Butts, *Dreams, "Evolution," and Value Fulfillment, Vol. 2* (New York: Prentice Hall Press, 1986), Session 910.

5. Jane Roberts, *The Seth Material* (New York: Prentice Hall Press, 1987), Appendix, p. 291.

6. Jane Roberts, *Seth Speaks: The Eternal Validity of the Soul* (San Rafael, Calif.: Amber-Allen/New World Library, 1994), Session 519.

7. Jane Roberts, *The Nature of Personal Reality* (San Rafael, Calif.: Amber-Allen/New World Library, 1994), Session 615.

8. Jane Roberts, *The "Unknown" Reality, Volume One* (San Rafael, Calif.: Amber-Allen Publishing, 1996), Session 679.

9. Jane Roberts, *The Individual and the Nature of Mass Events* (San Rafael, Calif.: Amber-Allen Publishing, 1995), Session 822.

10. Jane Roberts, *The Nature of the Psyche: Its Human Expression* (San Rafael, Calif.: Amber-Allen Publishing, 1996), Session 791.

11. Jane Roberts, *The Nature of the Psyche: Its Human Ex-*

pression (San Rafael, Calif.: Amber-Allen Publishing, 1996), Session 791.

12. Jane Roberts, Introductory Essays and Notes by Robert F. Butts, *Dreams, "Evolution," and Value Fulfillment, Vol. 2* (New York: Prentice Hall Press, 1986), Session 910.

13. Jane Roberts, *Seth Speaks: The Eternal Validity of the Soul* (San Rafael, Calif.: Amber-Allen/New World Library, 1994), Session 590.

14. Jane Roberts, *The Afterdeath Journal of an American Philosopher* (New York: Prentice Hall Press, 1987), Chapter 6, p. 113.

15. Jane Roberts, *The "Unknown" Reality, Volume One* (San Rafael, Calif.: Amber-Allen Publishing, 1996), Session 701.

16. Jane Roberts, *The Afterdeath Journal of an American Philosopher* (New York: Prentice Hall Press, 1987), Chapter 7, p. 119.

17. Jane Roberts, *The Nature of the Psyche: Its Human Expression* (San Rafael, Calif.: Amber-Allen Publishing, 1996), Session 800.

18. Jane Roberts, *The Nature of the Psyche: Its Human Expression* (San Rafael, Calif.: Amber-Allen Publishing, 1996), Session 800.

Chapter 5: Weaving the Web of Magic

1. Jane Roberts, *The Afterdeath Journal of an American Philosopher* (New York: Prentice Hall Press, 1987), Chapter 6, p. 124.

2. Jane Roberts, *The Nature of the Psyche: Its Human Expression* (San Rafael, Calif.: Amber-Allen Publishing, 1996), Session 789.

3. Jane Roberts, *The Nature of the Psyche: Its Human Expression* (San Rafael, Calif.: Amber-Allen Publishing, 1996), Session 789.

4. Jane Roberts, *The Nature of the Psyche: Its Human Expression* (San Rafael, Calif.: Amber-Allen Publishing, 1996), Session 789.

5. Jane Roberts, *The Nature of the Psyche: Its Human Expression* (San Rafael, Calif.: Amber-Allen Publishing, 1996), Session 789.

6. Jane Roberts, *Seth Speaks: The Eternal Validity of the Soul* (San Rafael, Calif.: Amber-Allen/New World Library, 1994), Session 581.

7. Jane Roberts, *Seth Speaks: The Eternal Validity of the Soul* (San Rafael, Calif.: Amber-Allen/New World Library, 1994), Session 524.

8. Jane Roberts, *Seth Speaks: The Eternal Validity of the Soul* (San Rafael, Calif.: Amber-Allen/New World Library, 1994), Session 525.

9. Jane Roberts, *The Individual and the Nature of Mass Events* (San Rafael, Calif.: Amber-Allen Publishing, 1995), Session 815.

10. Jane Roberts, *The Individual and the Nature of Mass Events* (San Rafael, Calif.: Amber-Allen Publishing, 1995), Session 825.

11. Jane Roberts, *The Nature of the Psyche: Its Human Expression* (San Rafael, Calif.: Amber-Allen Publishing, 1996), Session 800.

Chapter 6: The Inside Out Phenomenon
1. Jane Roberts, *Seth Speaks: The Eternal Validity of the Soul* (San Rafael, Calif.: Amber-Allen/New World Library, 1994), Session 520.

2. Jane Roberts, *The "Unknown" Reality, Volume Two* (San Rafael, Calif.: Amber-Allen Publishing, 1996), Session 727.

3. Jane Roberts, *Seth Speaks: The Eternal Validity of the Soul* (San Rafael, Calif.: Amber-Allen/New World Library,

1994), Session 555.

4. Jane Roberts, *The "Unknown" Reality, Volume One* (San Rafael, Calif.: Amber-Allen Publishing, 1996), Session 690.

5. Jane Roberts, *Seth Speaks: The Eternal Validity of the Soul* (San Rafael, Calif.: Amber-Allen/New World Library, 1994), Session 582.

6. Jane Roberts, *The Nature of Personal Reality* (San Rafael, Calif.: Amber-Allen/New World Library, 1994), Session 626.

7. Jane Roberts, *The "Unknown" Reality, Volume Two* (San Rafael, Calif.: Amber-Allen Publishing, 1996), Session 705.

8. Jane Roberts, *The "Unknown" Reality, Volume One* (San Rafael, Calif.: Amber-Allen Publishing, 1996), Session 684.

9. Jane Roberts, *The Individual and the Nature of Mass Events* (San Rafael, Calif.: Amber-Allen Publishing, 1995), Session 826.

10. Jane Roberts, *Seth Speaks: The Eternal Validity of the Soul* (San Rafael, Calif.: Amber-Allen/New World Library, 1994), Appendix, ESP Class Session, January 5, 1971.

11. Jane Roberts, *Seth Speaks: The Eternal Validity of the Soul* (San Rafael, Calif.: Amber-Allen/New World Library, 1994), Session 520.

12. Jane Roberts, *The Nature of Personal Reality* (San Rafael, Calif.: Amber-Allen/New World Library, 1994), Session 626.

13. Jane Roberts, *The "Unknown" Reality, Volume Two* (San Rafael, Calif.: Amber-Allen Publishing, 1996), Session 707.

14. Jane Roberts, Introductory Essays and Notes by Robert F. Butts, *Dreams, "Evolution," and Value Fulfillment, Vol. 1* (New York: Prentice Hall Press, 1986), Session 895.

15. Jane Roberts, *The Individual and the Nature of Mass Events* (San Rafael, Calif.: Amber-Allen Publishing, 1995), Session 822.

16. Jane Roberts, *The Afterdeath Journal of an American Philosopher* (New York: Prentice Hall Press, 1987), Chapter 15, p. 210.

17. Jane Roberts, *How to Develop Your ESP Power* (Hollywood, Florida: Lifetime Books, Inc., 1993), Chapter 14, p. 243.

18. Jane Roberts, *The Nature of the Psyche: Its Human Expression* (San Rafael, Calif.: Amber-Allen Publishing, 1996), Session 792.

19. Jane Roberts, *Seth, Dreams and Projections of Consciousness* (Walpole, N.H.: Stillpoint Publishing, 1986), Chapter 14, p. 238.

20. Jane Roberts, *The Nature of the Psyche: Its Human Expression* (San Rafael, Calif.: Amber-Allen Publishing, 1996), Session 792.

21. Jane Roberts, *Seth Speaks: The Eternal Validity of the Soul* (San Rafael, Calif.: Amber-Allen/New World Library, 1994), Session 535.

22. Jane Roberts, *The "Unknown" Reality, Volume Two* (San Rafael, Calif.: Amber-Allen Publishing, 1996), Session 708.

23. Jane Roberts, *The Individual and the Nature of Mass Events* (San Rafael, Calif.: Amber-Allen Publishing, 1995), Session 801.

24. Jane Roberts, *The Individual and the Nature of Mass Events* (San Rafael, Calif.: Amber-Allen Publishing, 1995), Session 801.

25. Jane Roberts, *The "Unknown" Reality, Volume One* (San Rafael, Calif.: Amber-Allen Publishing, 1996), Session 685.

26. Jane Roberts, *Seth Speaks: The Eternal Validity of the Soul* (San Rafael, Calif.: Amber-Allen/New World Library,

1994), Session 518.

27. Jane Roberts, Introductory Essays and Notes by Robert F. Butts, *Dreams, "Evolution," and Value Fulfillment, Vol. 1* (New York: Prentice Hall Press, 1986), Session 898.

Chapter 7: To Be or Not to Be...Is a Probability Selection

1. Jane Roberts, Introductory Essays and Notes by Robert F. Butts, *Dreams, "Evolution," and Value Fulfillment, Vol. 1* (New York: Prentice Hall Press, 1986), Session 897.

2. Jane Roberts, *How to Develop Your ESP Power* (Hollywood, Florida: Lifetime Books, Inc., 1993), Chapter 4, p. 67.

3. Jane Roberts, *How to Develop Your ESP Power* (Hollywood, Florida: Lifetime Books, Inc., 1993), Chapter 10, p. 172.

4. Jane Roberts, *The "Unknown" Reality, Volume Two* (San Rafael, Calif.: Amber-Allen Publishing, 1996), Session 709.

5. Jane Roberts, *The Nature of Personal Reality* (San Rafael, Calif.: Amber-Allen/New World Library, 1994), Session 654.

6. Jane Roberts, *The "Unknown" Reality, Volume One* (San Rafael, Calif.: Amber-Allen Publishing, 1996), Session 694.

7. Jane Roberts, *The Seth Material* (New York: Prentice Hall Press, 1987), Chapter 10, p. 113-4.

8. Norman Friedman, *Bridging Science and Spirit* (St. Louis: Living Lake Books, 1994), Chapter 11, p. 289.

9. Jane Roberts, *How to Develop Your ESP Power* (Hollywood, Florida: Lifetime Books, Inc., 1993), Chapter 11, p. 192.

10. Jane Roberts, *The Nature of the Psyche: Its Human Expression* (San Rafael, Calif.: Amber-Allen Publishing, 1996), Session 793.

11. Jane Roberts, *The "Unknown" Reality, Volume One* (San Rafael, Calif.: Amber-Allen Publishing, 1996), Session 687.

12. Jane Roberts, *The "Unknown" Reality, Volume Two* (San

Rafael, Calif.: Amber-Allen Publishing, 1996), Session 729.

13. Jane Roberts, *The Nature of Personal Reality* (San Rafael, Calif.: Amber-Allen/New World Library, 1994), Session 656.

14. Jane Roberts, *Seth, Dreams and Projections of Consciousness* (Walpole, N.H.: Stillpoint Publishing, 1986), Chapter 16, p. 275.

15. Jane Roberts, *Seth, Dreams and Projections of Consciousness* (Walpole, N.H.: Stillpoint Publishing, 1986), Chapter 18, p. 313.

16. Jane Roberts, *Seth, Dreams and Projections of Consciousness* (Walpole, N.H.: Stillpoint Publishing, 1986), Chapter 18, p. 313.

17. Jane Roberts, *Seth Speaks: The Eternal Validity of the Soul* (San Rafael, Calif.: Amber-Allen/New World Library, 1994), Session 565.

18. Jane Roberts, *Seth, Dreams and Projections of Consciousness* (Walpole, N.H.: Stillpoint Publishing, 1986), Chapter 18, p. 313.

19. Jane Roberts, *Seth, Dreams and Projections of Consciousness* (Walpole, N.H.: Stillpoint Publishing, 1986), Chapter 18, p. 313.

20. Jane Roberts, *The Seth Material* (New York: Prentice Hall Press, 1987), Chapter 9, p. 106.

21. Jane Roberts, *The "Unknown" Reality, Volume Two* (San Rafael, Calif.: Amber-Allen Publishing, 1996), Session 741.

22. Jane Roberts, *Seth Speaks: The Eternal Validity of the Soul* (San Rafael, Calif.: Amber-Allen/New World Library, 1994), Session 566.

23. Jane Roberts, *The Nature of Personal Reality* (San Rafael, Calif.: Amber-Allen/New World Library, 1994), Session 656.

24. Jane Roberts, *The Nature of Personal Reality* (San Rafael, Calif.: Amber-Allen/New World Library, 1994), Session 656.

25. Jane Roberts, *The Nature of Personal Reality* (San Rafael,

Calif.: Amber-Allen/New World Library, 1994), Session 655.

26. Jane Roberts, *The "Unknown" Reality, Volume One* (San Rafael, Calif.: Amber-Allen Publishing, 1996), Session 681.

27. Jane Roberts, *The Individual and the Nature of Mass Events* (San Rafael, Calif.: Amber-Allen Publishing, 1995), Session 827.

28. Jane Roberts, *The "Unknown" Reality, Volume Two* (San Rafael, Calif.: Amber-Allen Publishing, 1996), Session 741.

29. Jane Roberts, *The "Unknown" Reality, Volume Two* (San Rafael, Calif.: Amber-Allen Publishing, 1996), Appendix 23.

Chapter 8: The Wizards of Consciousness

1. Jane Roberts, *Seth Speaks: The Eternal Validity of the Soul* (San Rafael, Calif.: Amber-Allen/New World Library, 1994), Session 523.

2. Jane Roberts, *The Nature of Personal Reality* (San Rafael, Calif.: Amber-Allen/New World Library, 1994), Session 656.

3. Jane Roberts, *The "Unknown" Reality, Volume Two* (San Rafael, Calif.: Amber-Allen Publishing, 1996), Session 708.

4. Jane Roberts, *The Nature of the Psyche: Its Human Expression* (San Rafael, Calif.: Amber-Allen Publishing, 1996), Session 792.

5. Jane Roberts, Introductory Essays and Notes by Robert F. Butts, *Dreams, "Evolution," and Value Fulfillment, Vol. 1* (New York: Prentice Hall Press, 1986), Session 895.

6. Jane Roberts, *The Individual and the Nature of Mass Events* (San Rafael, Calif.: Amber-Allen Publishing, 1995), Session 824, Notes.

7. Jane Roberts, *The Nature of Personal Reality* (San Rafael, Calif.: Amber-Allen/New World Library, 1994), Session 654.

8. Jane Roberts, *Seth Speaks: The Eternal Validity of the Soul* (San Rafael, Calif.: Amber-Allen/New World Library, 1994), Session 523.

9. Jane Roberts, *The Nature of the Psyche: Its Human Ex-*

9. Jane Roberts, *The Nature of the Psyche: Its Human Expression* (San Rafael, Calif.: Amber-Allen Publishing, 1996), Session 797.

10. Jane Roberts, *The Nature of Personal Reality* (San Rafael, Calif.: Amber-Allen/New World Library, 1994), Session 654.

11. Jane Roberts, *Seth Speaks: The Eternal Validity of the Soul* (San Rafael, Calif.: Amber-Allen/New World Library, 1994), Session 582.

Chapter 9: High Stepping Into the Future

1. Jane Roberts, *Seth Speaks: The Eternal Validity of the Soul* (San Rafael, Calif.: Amber-Allen/New World Library, 1994), Session 523.

2. Jane Roberts, *Psychic Politics* (Englewood Cliffs, N.J.: Prentice-Hall, Inc., 1976), Chapter 16, p. 203.

3. Jane Roberts, *Seth Speaks: The Eternal Validity of the Soul* (San Rafael, Calif.: Amber-Allen/New World Library, 1994), Session 582.

4. Jane Roberts, *Seth Speaks: The Eternal Validity of the Soul* (San Rafael, Calif.: Amber-Allen/New World Library, 1994), Session 591.

5. Jane Roberts, *Seth Speaks: The Eternal Validity of the Soul* (San Rafael, Calif.: Amber-Allen/New World Library, 1994), Appendix, p. 405.

6. Jane Roberts, *The Seth Material* (New York: Prentice Hall Press, 1987), Chapter 18, p. 247.

7. Jane Roberts, *The Magical Approach* (San Rafael, Calif.: Amber-Allen/New World Library, 1995), Session 2, p. 17.

8. Jane Roberts, *The Magical Approach* (San Rafael, Calif.: Amber-Allen/New World Library, 1995), Session 3, p. 28.

9. Jane Roberts, *The Magical Approach* (San Rafael, Calif.: Amber-Allen/New World Library, 1995), Session 7, p. 70.

10. Susan M. Watkins, *Conversations With Seth, Vol. 2* (New York: Prentice Hall Press, 1981), Chapter 13, p. 340.

11.   From the unpublished session recorded on December 9, 1981.

12.   Jane Roberts, *Psychic Politics* (Englewood Cliffs, N.J.: Prentice-Hall, Inc., 1976), Chapter 21, p. 264.

13.   Jane Roberts, *Seth Speaks: The Eternal Validity of the Soul* (San Rafael, Calif.: Amber-Allen/New World Library, 1994), Session 586.

14.   Jane Roberts, *The "Unknown" Reality, Volume One* (San Rafael, Calif.: Amber-Allen Publishing, 1996), Session 688.

15.   Jane Roberts, *The Individual and the Nature of Mass Events* (San Rafael, Calif.: Amber-Allen Publishing, 1995), Session 873.

16.   Jane Roberts, *The Individual and the Nature of Mass Events* (San Rafael, Calif.: Amber-Allen Publishing, 1995), Session 873.

Suggested Reading

Books by Jane Roberts, Dictated by Seth

Roberts, Jane. *Seth Speaks: The Eternal Validity of the Soul.* Notes by Robert F. Butts. San Rafael, Calif.: Amber-Allen/New World Library, 1994.

___. *The Nature of Personal Reality: A Seth Book.* Notes by Robert F. Butts. San Rafael, Calif.: Amber-Allen/New World Library, 1994.

___. *The "Unknown" Reality: A Seth Book, Volume One.* Notes and Introduction by Robert F. Butts. San Rafael, Calif.: Amber-Allen Publishing, 1996.

___. *The "Unknown" Reality: A Seth Book, Volume Two.* Notes and Introduction by Robert F. Butts. San Rafael, Calif.: Amber-Allen Publishing, 1996.

___. *The Nature of the Psyche: Its Human Expression.* San Rafael, Calif.: Amber-Allen Publishing, 1996.

___. *The Individual and the Nature of Mass Events.* Notes by Robert F. Butts. San Rafael, Calif.: Amber-Allen Publishing, 1995.

___. *Dreams, "Evolution," and Value Fulfillment, Volume One.* Introductory Essays and Notes by Robert F. Butts. New York: Prentice Hall Press, 1986.

___. *Dreams, "Evolution," and Value Fulfillment, Volume Two.* Introductory Essays and Notes by Robert F. Butts. New York: Prentice Hall Press, 1986.

___. *The Magical Approach: Seth Speaks About the Art of Creative Living.* Notes by Robert F. Butts. San Rafael, Calif.: Amber-Allen/New World Library, 1995.

Books by Jane Roberts, Related to Her Work With Seth

Roberts, Jane. *How to Develop Your ESP Power*. Hollywood, Florida: Lifetime Books, Inc., 1993.

___. *The Seth Material*. New York: Prentice Hall Press, 1970.

___. *Adventures in Consciousness: An Introduction to Aspect Psychology*. New York: Bantam Books, 1975. (To be republished by SethNet Publishing, Eugene, Ore., in 1997.)

___. *Dialogues of the Soul and Mortal Self in Time*. Englewood Cliffs, N.J.: Prentice-Hall, Inc., 1975.

___. *Psychic Politics: An Aspect Psychology Book*. Englewood Cliffs, N.J.: Prentice-Hall, Inc., 1976. (To be republished by SethNet Publishing, Eugene, Ore., in 1997.)

___. *The World View of Paul Cezanne*. Englewood Cliffs, N.J.: Prentice-Hall, Inc., 1977.

___. *The Afterdeath Journal of an American Philosopher: The World View of William James*. New York: Prentice Hall Press, 1978.

___. *Emir's Education in the Proper Use of Magical Powers*. Walpole, N.H.: Stillpoint Publishing, 1984.

___. *The God of Jane: A Psychic Manifesto*. Englewood Cliffs, N.J.: Prentice-Hall, Inc., 1981. (To be republished by SethNet Publishing, Eugene, Ore., in 1998.)

___. *If We Live Again: Or, Public Magic and Private Love*. New York: Prentice Hall Press, 1982.

___. *Seth, Dreams and Projections of Consciousness*. Walpole, N.H.: Stillpoint Publishing, 1986.

___. *The Oversoul Seven Trilogy: The Education of Oversoul Seven; The Further Education of Oversoul Seven; Oversoul Seven and the Museum of Time*. San Rafael, Calif.: Amber-Allen Publishing, 1995.

Additional Authors

Ashley, Nancy. *Create Your Own Reality: A Seth Workbook.* New York: Prentice Hall Press, 1987. (To be republished by SethNet Publishing, Eugene, Ore., in 1997.)

___. *Create Your Own Happiness: A Seth Workbook.* New York: Prentice Hall Press, 1988. (To be republished by SethNet Publishing, Eugene, Ore., in 1997.)

___. *Create Your Own Dreams: A Seth Workbook.* New York: Prentice Hall Press, 1990. (To be republished by SethNet Publishing, Eugene, Ore., in 1998.)

Barton, Mary. *Soul Sight.* (To be published by SethNet Publishing, Eugene, Ore., in 1997.)

Friedman, Norman. *Bridging Science and Spirit: Common Elements in David Bohm's Physics, The Perennial Philosophy and Seth.* Eugene, Ore.: The Woodbridge Group, 1997.

___. *The Hidden Domain.* Eugene, Ore.: The Woodbridge Group, 1997.

Hay, Louise. *You Can Heal Your Body.* Carlsbad, Calif.: Hay House, Inc., 1982.

___. *You Can Heal Your Life.* Carlsbad, Calif.: Hay House, Inc., 1984.

Mawe, Sheelagh. *Dandelion: The Triumphant Life of a Misfit.* Orlando, Florida: Totally Unique Thoughts, 1987.

McDonald, John. *The Message of a Master.* San Rafael, Calif.: New World Library, 1993.

Perl, Sheri. *Healing From the Inside Out.* New York: NAL Penguin, Inc., 1988. (To be republished by SethNet Publishing, Eugene, Ore., in 1997.)

Stack, Rick. *Out-of-Body Adventures: 30 Days to the Most Exciting Experience of Your Life.* Chicago: Contemporary Books, Inc., 1988.

Stone, Christopher. *Re-Creating Your Self.* Carlsbad, Calif.: Hay House, Inc., 1990.

Sheldon, Mary, and Christopher Stone. *The Meditation Journal.*
West Hollywood, Calif.: Dove Books, 1996.
Watkins, Susan M. *Conversations With Seth: The Story of Jane
Roberts's ESP Class, Volume One.* New York: Prentice Hall Press,
1986. (To be republished by SethNet Publishing, Eugene, Ore.,
in 1997.)
___. *Conversations With Seth: The Story of Jane Roberts's ESP Class,
Volume Two.* New York: Prentice Hall Press, 1986. (To be
republished by SethNet Publishing, Eugene, Ore., in 1997.)
___. *Dreaming Myself, Dreaming a Town.* New York: Kendall
Enterprises, Inc., 1989. (To be republished by SethNet
Publishing, Eugene, Ore., in 1998.)

Stan Ulkowski

About the Author

Lynda Dahl is president and chair of the Board of Directors of Seth Network International; vice president of The Woodbridge Group; and author of *Beyond the Winning Streak: Using Conscious Creation to Consistently Win at Life*, and *Ten Thousand Whispers: A Guide to Conscious Creation*. A former computer industry vice president, she now lectures extensively on consciousness and has appeared on numerous radio and television shows. Lynda's immediate family includes her partner Stan Ulkowski, children Matthew and Cathleen, and cats galore.

SETH NETWORK INTERNATIONAL

Seth Network International (SNI) is a network of Seth/Jane Roberts readers from over 30 countries who meet to explore the ideas and share the excitement of the Seth material. SNI, a nonprofit company established in late 1992, provides the meeting place, or forum, for the gathering. Its primary purpose is to offer Seth readers a platform for expression and discussion.

SNI publishes a quarterly magazine, *Reality Change: The Global Seth Journal*; holds conferences each year; and offers The Brass Ring Bookstore, a mail-order catalog filled with Seth/Jane Roberts books, art, audiotapes and videotapes, and products by other authors. In 1996 SethNet Publishing, a division of SNI, was formed to publish some of Jane Roberts's books and other books compatible with the concepts found in the Seth material.

You can find SNI on CompuServe (GO NEWAAGE), where an on-line conference is held weekly at 6:30 p.m. Pacific Standard Time, and where you can peruse a library of Seth-related articles and follow ongoing discussions on the message board. On SNI's World Wide Web home page you will find almost 100 screens of information on the latest happenings around the Seth material and Seth Network International (http://www.efn.org/~sethweb). For The Brass Ring Bookstore catalog or further information, please contact:

Seth Network International
PO Box 1620
Eugene, OR 97440 USA
Phone (541) 683-0803 Fax (541) 683-1084